Shalom

Kirk House Publishers

Shalom

Our search for peace
in a troubled world

Terry R. Morehouse

Shalom: Our search for peace in a troubled world
© Copyright 2021 Terry R Morehouse

First Edition
ISBN: 9781952976216
Library of Congress Control Number: 2021914099

Cover photo, design and interior design: Ann Aubitz

Published by Kirk House Publishers
1250 E 115th Street
Burnsville, MN 55337
Kirkhousepublishers.com
612-781-2815

In Memory of Our Parents
Roy And Irene Morehouse and
Svea Elizabeth And C. Ernest Carlstrom
To whom we shall ever be grateful.

SHALOM
OUR SEARCH FOR PEACE
IN A TROUBLED WORLD

*"The beautiful Jewish greeting, 'Shalom,' wishes you
the fullness of divine promise. It prays that you may
possess all the qualities that fulfill the human condition, rather than any circumstance that may wreck it.'"*
(J.J. Greehy, Mary the Mother of God, commentary)

Dear Fellow Travelers,

Well, here I am, hunkered into our little cabin by the shores
of old Sand Lake in northeastern Minnesota. What am I doing
here? Who knows exactly? What do I want to accomplish here?
I'm not really sure. But it's the end of a significant chapter for me.
In March of 2021, I turned 80 years old. Twenty-six years ago, I
was asked to do a weekly radio broadcast for Mount Olivet Lutheran Church. Consider this book my way of saying thank you
to all who have listened.

In some ways, I've always been searching for peace in our
troubled world. Why not continue the journey, I reasoned? Life

is, after all, about the journey. Life isn't about winning or losing. It's about taking a step of faith, and then another, as long as we can.

As President Jimmy Carter once said, "My faith demands—this is not optional—my faith demands that I do whatever I can, wherever I can, whenever I can, for as long as I can, with whatever I have, to try to make a difference."

I may not have much. I could easily be accused of giving in to the temptation of "diddling around in the contemplative life," as Annie Dillard once wrote. In some respects, I've always been a diddler. But the way I look at it, if I'm destined to be a diddler, I might as well diddle around in a pursuit for peace.

Many of these offerings started out, or were included, in a radio broadcast. Others began in the silences of my private reveries. Thank you for joining me as together we search for peace in our troubled world.

Terry R. Morehouse, 2021

TABLE OF CONTENTS

SECTION 1 - MAKE ME AN INSTRUMENT OF YOUR PEACE

SECTION 2 - SAINTS AND SINNERS

SECTION 3 - REFLECTIONS THROUGH THE YEAR

SECTION 4 - LEAVES FROM A PASTOR'S NOTEBOOK

ACKNOWLEDGEMENTS

Grateful acknowledgement is made to the following authors, publishers and other copyright holders for the use of material quoted in this book, many of whom are included in the text itself. If any material has been used without proper credit, please notify the author so that proper credit can be given.

Scriptural quotations have been taken from the New Revised Standard Version of the Bible, copyright 1989, by the Division of Christian Education of the National Churches of Christ in the U.S.A., Thomas Nelson Inc., Nashville, Tenn. Hymn texts are from the Evangelical Lutheran Worship, Augsburg Fortress, 2006

- From a speech by David Dwight Eisenhower, April 16, 1953
- From "Beyond Words" by Frederick Beuchner, Harper/Collins. 1989
- From "The Prophet" by Kahlil Gibran, Alfred Knopf, 1951
- From "Make Me an Instrument of Your Peace", Kent Nerbern, by Harper Collins Publishers, NY

- From "Left to Tell" by Immaculee Ilibagiza, Hayhouse Inc. Carlsbad, Cal, 2006
- From "Stories from the Heart," edited by Alice Gray, Multnomah Book, Sisters, Ore.
- From "Daily Study Bible" by William Barclay, Westminster Press, 1956
- From "Reflections on the Peace Prayer of St. Francis of Assisi," by Albert Haase, O.F.M., St. Anthony Messenger Press, Cincinnati, Oh., 2004
- From "Evangelical Lutheran Worship," Augsburg Fortress, 2006, Evangelical Lutheran Church in America
- From "The Courage Center" Newsletter, Golden Valley, Minn.
- From "The Cost of Discipleship" by Dietrich Bonhoeffer, Collier, McMillan Publishing, 1937
- From "Speaking in Stories" by William White, Augsburg, 1982
- From "David Cleary," attorney, with personal permission
- From "Wishful Thinking" by Frederick Beuchner, Harper and Row, New York, 1973
- From "Guerillas of Grace" by Ted Loder, Augsburg Fortress, 2005
- From "Christmas in My Soul," edited by Joe Wheeler, written by Nancy Rue, for Focus on the Family, Dec. 1998
- From "Christian Century Magazine," July 2007
- From "Stories and Reflections for Sunday Readings," by Megan McKenna, Orbis Books, Maryknoll, NY, 1998

- From "A Tree Grows in Brooklyn," by Betty Smith, Harper/Collins, NY
- From "Sundays and Seasons 2020," by David Miller, Augsburg/Fortress
- From "Lent: The Sunday Readings" by Megan McKenna, Orbis Books, Maryknoll, NY, 1997
- From "The Hungering Dark" by Frederick Beuchner, The Seabury Press, 1969
- From "The Measure of our Success" by Marian Wright Edelman
- From "The Clergy Journal" by Walter Brueggeman, May/June 2001
- From "The Future, lyrics by Leonard Cohen, "There's a Crack in Everything."
- From "Psalms for the Sojourner" by James Limburg, Augsburg, Minneapolis, 1986
- From "The Washington Post Weekly" February 7, 2021, Washington, D.C. 20071
- From "Alive Now" by Andrea Woods, Sept./Oct. 2008
- From Minneapolis Star/Tribune, op/ed by Scott Bengston, August 2020
- From "Wheels in the Air" by William Joyner, United Church Press,1968
- From "Fiddler on the Roof"
- From Poem with personal permission, "To Joyce and Clarence Pederson"

My special thanks and recognition to my life-long partner of 57 years, **Joan Morehouse,** for her constant encouragement, patience, and love. (Most of the photos included in this book were taken by her.) To **Susan Haberle**, my diligent and meticulous editor of this and two of my other publications.

Also to the members and friends of **Mount Olivet Lutheran Church, Minneapolis, Minnesota; Trinity Lutheran Church, Princeton, Minnesota; Bethany College, Lindsborg, Kansas; Faith Evangelical Lutheran Church, Waconia, Minnesota; Lyndale Lutheran Church, Maple Plain, Minnesota; and Trinity Lutheran Church, Kenosha, Wisconsin.** Additional thanks to **David Lose**, senior pastor of Mount Olivet Lutheran Church, to all of my pastoral colleagues and the staff there, as well as the many "Fellow Travelers" along the way who have shared the journey with me.

Also, thanks to my daughter, **Amy Abrahamson**, for her help in so many matters of computer technology, to my sister-in-law **Mary Strand** for her constant encouragement and support, and to **Ann Aubitz** of Kirk House Publishers, Burnsville, Minnesota. It's been a great ride!

Note: All poetry unless otherwise specified was written by the author, at various points during his ministry.

Terry R. Morehouse

SECTION 1
MAKE ME AN INSTRUMENT
OF YOUR PEACE

Lord, make me an instrument of your peace. That where there is hatred, let me sow love; where there is injury, pardon; where there is doubt, faith; where there is despair, hope; where there is darkness, light; where there is sadness, joy.

Help me not so much to be consoled, as to console; to be understood, as to understand; to be loved, as to love.

For it is in giving that we receive. It is in forgiving that we are forgiven. It is in dying, that we are born to eternal life.

(Anonymous, often attributed to St. Francis of Assisi)

Chapter 1

MAKE ME AN INSTRUMENT
OF YOUR PEACE

"Many peoples shall come and say, 'Come, let us go up to the mountain of the Lord, to the house of the God of Jacob, that he may teach us his ways, and that we may walk in his paths.' For out of Zion shall go forth instruction and the word of the Lord from Jerusalem. He shall judge between the nations, and shall arbitrate for many peoples; they shall beat their swords into plowshares, and their spears into pruning hooks; nation shall not lift up sword against nation, neither shall they learn war anymore." (Isaiah 2:3-4)

Standing just to the right of the tomb of one of the most beloved presidents of our nation are the following words: "Every gun made, every warship launched, every rocket fired signifies, in the final sense, a theft from those who hunger and are not fed, those who are cold and are not clothed. This is not a way of life at all…under the cloud of threatening war, it is humanity, hanging from a cross of iron." (President Dwight D. Eisenhower)

I have dedicated this next section of our book to what has come to be known as a "Prayer for Peace."

There are some ironies here as we begin these next few chapters. The first is that we began with a quotation from one of the greatest military generals our nation has ever known. The quote from former president Eisenhower came from a speech he gave to the American Society of Newspaper Editors on April 16, 1953, shortly after the death of Joseph Stalin. "Ike," as he came to be known and loved, is often credited with leading the world through one of the most dangerous times in history. He was, of course, the allied commander in chief during the second World War. It was he who strategically and seemingly confidently and successfully led the allied forces to defeat the powerful war machine in Nazi Germany under the leadership of Adolf Hitler.

So, we began with a message of peace from a man who knew war as intimately as any leader has ever known.

The second great irony is that this same prayer, this "Prayer for Peace," with which this section begins, has often been credited to St. Francis of Assisi, a diminutive little Christian friar and leader of the Brothers of the Poor in 13th century Europe.

The more I learned about the life of Francesco Bernardoni, better known as St. Francis of Assisi, it wasn't too hard to understand why this prayer has been attached to his name, despite the fact that he lived some 700 years before the prayer first appeared in print.

Love was the key to understanding this little man who gave himself to Jesus Christ. And so, love must be at the center of our search for peace in our troubled world.

St. Francis settled disputes between the Bishop of Assisi and its mayor. He spoke before kings, royalty, and popes, while clinging steadfastly to his vow of poverty. In his travels, the little friar would pick up worms along his path in order not to step on them. He loved the entire universe. The sun, the moon, the fire, as well as the insects and stones along the road. Francis believed that we cannot separate human life from the life of the air or land or water, a lesson we are desperately still trying to learn. In short, even though he couldn't possibly have written this prayer since he lived so long before the prayer ever appeared in writing, his life was a life of peace, so it is no wonder that the prayer has been attributed to him.

"Lord make me an instrument of your peace," the prayer begins.

Prayers for peace have long been on the hearts and minds of people of all nationalities and all religions. Yet that same peace for which we pray always seems to be just beyond our grasp. "They shall beat their swords into plowshares, and their spears into pruning hooks," Isaiah wrote in our text for this message. "Nation shall not lift up sword against nation, neither shall they learn war anymore." Yet even today, and perhaps especially today, Isaiah's dream seems so far away.

Yet still we pray, "Lord make me an instrument of your peace."

Writes the author Frederick Beuchner, "Peace has come to mean a time when there aren't any wars or even when there aren't any major wars. Most of us would settle for that. But in Hebrew, peace, shalom, means 'fullness,' means having everything you need to be wholly and happily yourself."

So, in our search for peace, we must begin with ourselves, yet we cannot stop there, always looking beyond ourselves. Our search for peace must begin in our homes, with how we treat those nearest and dearest to us. "Violence," Jesuit peace activist John Dear tells us, "occurs when we forget and deny our basic identity as God's children; when we treat one another as if we were worthless instead of priceless."

The practice of peace involves introspection. "If you love peace," says Mahatma Gandhi, the world's foremost advocate for non-violence, "then hate injustice, hate tyranny, hate greed—but hate these things inside yourself, not in another."

The practice of peace continues in our nation, in our communities, in our neighborhoods, and at work, where our sense of community has grown tattered and frail. Nobel Peace Prize recipient Mother Teresa brings to mind what is at stake here. "If we have no peace, it is because we have forgotten that we belong to each other," she said.

"Lord make me an instrument of your peace."

When we pray this beautiful prayer, may each of us begin by bowing down before God and humbly offering ourselves up to the Great Musician, then allowing our own instrument to be heard, as humble and as insignificant as our gift might seem to be. We must offer ourselves to be shaped into a form through which the voice of God can be heard.

To pray this prayer would be a wonderful way to begin each day.

♦   ♦   ♦

Let us pray: "Lord make me an instrument of your peace. Let peace be my fervent prayer, and let it begin with me." Amen.

Chapter 2

WHERE THERE IS HATRED,
LET ME SOW LOVE

*"But strive for the greater gifts. And I will still show you
a more excellent way." (I Corinthians 12:31)*

These words from St. Paul's first letter to the Corinthians are, of course, the great apostle's introduction to what has come to be called "the love chapter" of the New Testament. This still more excellent way is the way of love.

The way of love is at the heart of our prayer for peace. "Where there is hatred, let me sow love," we pray.

Sounds pretty easy, huh? I mean, who could have anything against love? Yet, when all is said and done, this part of our prayer may be the hardest of all. According to St. Paul, when love is set beside all of the spiritual gifts that God has given his church, it is the greatest gift of all.

Through the years of my ministry, I have made it a point to meet with young couples who tell me they have fallen in love.

They are surprised when I tell them that may be the very reason they should *not* get married! Oh, I want them to love each other. I am a true romantic at heart. But by describing love as something you fall into or out of seems to me to miss the very essence of what love is all about.

Listen again to the words of that beautiful chapter in Corinthians:

"Love is patient; love is kind;
Love is not envious or boastful, or arrogant, or rude.
It does not insist on its own way; it is not irritable or resentful;
It does not rejoice in wrong doing, but rejoices in the truth.
It bears all things, believes all things, hopes all things,
Endures all things. Love never ends."

We pray in our prayer for peace, "where there is hatred, let me sow love." Deep within the wisdom of this prayer, the author understands the human heart. The author knows that love is stronger than hate because hate is an active, predatory force, proceeding from an empty center. A love, even the most fragile, can conquer hate, because the empty center at the core of hate is always silently crying out to be filled with love.

I have always deeply admired the gift that poets have for expressing such things as these. The Persian poet Gibran has this to say about love:

"When love beckons to you, follow him though his ways be hard and steep
And though his wings enfold you, yield to him,

Though the sword hidden among his pinions may wound you.
And when he speaks to you, believe in him,
Though his voice may shatter your dreams as the north wind lays
waste the garden.

"For even as love crowns you, so shall he crucify you. Even as he is
for your growth, so is he for your pruning. Even as he ascends to your
height and caresses your tenderest branches that quiver in the sun, So,
shall he descend to your roots and shake them in their clinging to the
earth." (The Prophet)

The way of love goes far beyond a moonlight night with snowflakes falling down around us. As much as we might wish it to be true, those two beautiful people we see with stars in their eyes on the Hallmark channel are a long, long way from what love is really all about. The way of love can never be just between two people. Loving ourselves can often be the hardest job of all.

When in this prayer we ask the Lord and master of our lives to help us *sow* love instead of hatred, we are not presuming that our lives will automatically manifest love in full flower. We pray that we will be given the courage to plant the seed, and that someone will pick us up whenever we fall. We need a far greater power than we can somehow muster on our own. Only by God's grace can we even come close to discovering the full meaning of this prayer.

Love is a habit of the heart that is not afraid to challenge the darkness inside us and around it. Even a small flowering of love can continue to grow, if it is tended carefully, and it can become a part of the legacy that we carry with us as we move through life. So be gentle with yourself. And remember, the only perfect love that we have ever seen came long ago, on a desolate hillside, where there was a man gasping for his breath, because of you.

There is peace here, in this cross, for our troubled world. Thank God.

◆　◆　◆

Let us pray: You have shown us a "more excellent way," O Lord, as your love became flesh and lived among us. May we be given whatever it takes to let that same love live in our lives. Amen.

Chapter 3
WHERE THERE IS INJURY,
LET ME SOW PARDON

"Be merciful, just as your Father is merciful. Do not judge, and you will not be judged; do not condemn, and you will not be condemned. Forgive, and you will be forgiven." (Luke 6:36-37)

As we seek to find shalom for ourselves and for others, we are reminded that we seldom find it on our own. Shalom is rarely found in isolation.

We might prefer not to muddy the waters of our peace by having to face it by looking into the eyes of those with whom we must live in this place.

It's so much easier to simply find a quiet place to be alone – alone with God, alone in nature's quiet beauty, alone in the starry vastness of the universe. There is something soothing about simply following the yearnings of our heart, to go deep into the woods like Thoreau. We love those quiet places in our lives, when we can walk barefoot by the sea, losing ourselves in the rhythm of the pounding waves, leaving the world behind. We need those quiet places, to let them wrap their arms around us, to soothe us in their quietude and comfort.

Our "Prayer for Peace" reminds us that as tempting as it may be to try to lose ourselves, to step beyond the communities we are bound to live in, we cannot spend our lives there. The peace that so many of us are looking for will always challenge us to face the people in our lives – the people, with all their warts and wrinkles, lumps and bumps that look so remarkably like our own.

"Where there is injury, let me sow pardon." That's the hard part. This was never meant to be a simple and an easy prayer - only a prayer that will lead to peace.

Are we to forgive all manner of crimes and transgressions? Are we being called to achieve some elevated state of spiritual enlightenment in which we can accept the evils of the world as somehow reflecting a higher purpose? Or is this petition of our prayer the blithe platitude of someone who has lived an unencumbered life on this earth?

The author Kent Nerburn, in his book of reflections on this prayer, has said, "If we are earnest seekers of the way of Christ in the world, these questions deserve our searching hearts. They admit to no easy answers."

Then he goes on to share his own experience that gave him insight into what some of those answers might be.

He tells about being present in a courtroom where a young man was on trial for murdering a girl he had seen walking down the street. He had not known her personally. She had not wronged him in any fashion whatsoever. He said her crime was simply being young and alive and in the wrong place at the wrong time. He described how he and a friend had dragged her into the woods, placed a gun behind her ear, and blown off the back of her head.

The prosecuting attorney described in grim detail the specifics of the murder and held up a bloody paper bag that contained the clothes of the young victim. Most in the courtroom averted their eyes. But through it all, the father of the murdered girl sat impassively, watching the trial, watching the boy.

After the trial was over, and the boy was found guilty, the father announced that he was going to visit the boy in jail and get to know him. People were appalled. Why would anyone who had suffered what this man had been suffering undertake such a task?

The father was insistent. "That boy and I are forever bound," he said. "We need to know each other. I do not know if I can forgive him. But perhaps if I know him, I will not hate him. This is about healing and reconciliation." ("Make Me an Instrument of Your Peace,"p.23)

When I read that story, I was pretty sure I would never have been able to do what that father wanted to do, even if in my heart of hearts, I knew that this may have been the only place where healing for either that young man or the girl's father could ever possibly begin. How could the father get over his rage? But this is not about giving approval, I knew. This is not about acceptance or an easy forgiveness. He could easily become lost in bitterness and hatred for the rest of his life and the life of that young man. He had sought, instead, to sow the seeds of healing for both of them.

"Where there is injury, let me sow pardon."

Deep within the wisdom of this prayer, there speaks the voice of the Lord and master of our lives. We see him there. On a cross. We hear his prayer, "Father, forgive them, for they know not what they are doing." This is not about making bitter memories disappear. The scars will always remain. Our "Prayer for Peace" urges us, instead, to sow the only seeds that can stop the bleeding that will last forever.

Some time ago, many of us at Mount Olivet were given the opportunity to meet and hear the story of Immaculee Ilibagiza, a young woman who lost most of her family during the 1994 genocide in Rwanda. More than a million ethnic Tutsis were slaughtered in fewer than three months after the death of their president. Immaculee's entire family, all except for her, were violently murdered.

When the slaughter finally ended, and she went to her homeland, she asked to see the leader of the gang who had mercilessly killed her family. When he entered the room, and he saw her standing before him, the color drained from his face. "His dirty clothing hung from his emaciated frame," she said. "His skin was sallow. I wept at the sight of his suffering." In her words, he had let the devil enter his heart, and the evil had ruined him like a cancer in his soul. He was now the victim of the victims, destined to live in torment and regret.

"Felician was sobbing," Immaculee wrote. "I could feel his shame. He looked up at me for just a moment, but our eyes met. I reached out, touched his hands lightly, and quietly said what I'd come to say. I forgive you." I saw the tension release in Felician's shoulders, as the police officer pushed him out the door. When the officer returned, he was furious. "What was all that about, Immaculee?" he demanded. "He murdered your family. I brought him to you to question, to spit on, if you wanted to. But you forgave him! How could you do that? Why did you forgive him?"

"I answered him with the truth," she said. "Forgiveness is all I have to offer." ("Left to Tell," Immaculee Ilibagiza, p. 204)

◆　◆　◆

Let us pray: So often we become lost in our bitterness and hatred, dear God, hanging onto hurts that have wounded us for far less cause than these. We may never forget. The scars will always be ours. Give us the gift of grace to sow seeds of pardon when we have been injured. That kind of forgiveness, that kind of peace, can only come from you, O Lord. It is not the way of the world, but it is your way for us, that someday, some way, we may at last find peace. In your name we pray. Amen.

Chapter 4

WHERE THERE IS DOUBT,
LET ME SOW FAITH

"And about three o'clock in the afternoon, Jesus cried with a loud voice, 'Eli, Eli, lama sabachtani,' that is, 'My God, my God, why have you forsaken me?'" (Matt. 27:46)

Our petition in this chapter is, once again, one that may not come easily for most of us. "Where there is doubt, let me sow faith."

Sowing faith in the midst of doubt is something many of us are reticent to do. For a lot of us, faith is a private thing. It's something each person must struggle with on his or her own. Who among us feels qualified to come up with answers to those deep-seated questions and doubts of others?

For one reason, at least, each of us has so many doubts of our own. We rarely take the risk of sounding so self-righteous or sure of ourselves that we would dare to tell others how or what or why to believe.

While I was thinking about all of this, I came across a couple of quotes that might surprise you. Here is the first:

"O all you who pass along the way, look and see if there is any sorrow like my sorrows. For many dogs surrounded me, a pack of evil doers closed in on me. They looked and stared at me; they divided my garments among them, and cast lots for my tunic.

"They pierced my hands and my feet; they counted all my bones. They opened their mouth against me, like a raging and roaring lion. I have been poured out like water, and all my bones have been scattered. My heart has become like a melting way, in the midst of my bosom. My strength has been dried up like baked clay, and my tongue clings to my jaw."

Written as a psalm, it comes to us by none other than **St. Francis of Assisi,** the man who has been credited with having written this beautiful "Prayer for Peace." Could there ever have been a more convincing model of faith than this dear man of the 13th century? Yet, here he is, in his own prayer, confessing his feelings of abandonment by God, his own utter and complete sense of isolation from the Lord and master of his life!

And here is the second quote.

"I call, I cling, I want—and there is no one to answer—no one to whom I can cling to, no one—alone. The darkness is so dark and I am alone—unwanted, forsaken. The loneliness of the heart that wants to love is unbearable

"In spite of it all—this darkness and emptiness is not as painful as the longing for God."

Published in 2007, those words were written by **Mother Te-resa**, Nobel Peace Prize laureate and on her way to sainthood in the Roman Catholic Church. When her private writings were first revealed, the world was shocked. "Surely," many of us thought, "this woman who had so radically impacted the world must always have lived in the radiant presence of God! How else could such a person as she live the lifestyle she lived, serving the poorest of the poor in the most inhumane conditions on earth?"

In spite of feelings like these, the miracle is that she continued to devote her life to others, even in the midst of them. The same could easily be said of Saint Francis, who shared his own feelings of abandonment by God in many prayers and psalms.

Then, there is Jesus, as he walked the lonely road to the cross. "My God, my God, why have you forsaken me?" (Matt. 27:46)

If we are completely honest, we, too, can identify periods in our own lives like theirs.

And so we pray, "Where there is doubt, let me sow faith."

Writes Kent Nerburn, "We must remember that more people live in the shadow of doubt, than in any blinding light of faith." ("Make Me an Instrument of Your Peace," p.37) As we seek to live out the words of our prayer, we cannot be afraid to share those times in our own lives, for all of us have gone through them. Each of us lives in the company of such giants as these.

In a poem that I wrote for my third book, "Traveling Home," I tried to express those feelings that I, too, have experienced. I called it, "At the Heart of Things."

Do you ever wonder why?
Do you ever wonder what the reason is?
For all of this?
Do you ever wonder if it pays—
To trust the living god,
To put your life behind a greater
Word than all the other words we hear?

I know I can't accept the simple answers.
Life has colored me that way.
Just because I dream of heaven,
Doesn't make it all OK

And yet, there IS a dream, I dream.
That at the heart of things
There is a mystery,
Deep beneath the places we shall ever go.
There is a holiness
Far beyond the holy places of the earth.
There is a love—beyond all human loving.

I trust in that. On my best days,
I believe.
And I pray, that on my worst days,
I'll be strengthened
In my unbelief. ("Traveling Home," p. 58)

♦ ♦ ♦

Let us pray: Enter the places of our own feelings of abandonment, dear God. May we openly stand beside others who have experienced the same. Let us stand together as we experience those "dark nights of our soul." Together, not with glibness, nor with quick and easy platitudes, but with a heart and mind that know those feelings as our own. We pray in your name. Amen.

Chapter 5

WHERE THERE IS DESPAIR,
LET ME SOW HOPE

"They went to a place called Gethsemane, and he said to his disciples, 'Sit here and wait while I pray.' He took with him Peter, and James, and John, and he began to be distressed and agitated. And he said to them, I am deeply grieved, even to death; remain here, and keep awake."
(Mark 14:32-34)

During the season of Lent, we, like the disciples of our Lord, seek to go where he goes, to follow him, even to the end, wherever that might be. Like his first disciples, we're not always very good at that. It's a daily battle, this journey of ours, and all too often we lose the way.

There are lots of different reasons for that. Our Jesus is not always the easiest Lord to follow in life, for one thing. His demands are many, it seems. We run out of gas. We fall asleep. We succumb to our own human weakness and fear.

Our text today takes us to the garden of Gethsemane. It's the night before the end of Jesus' life on earth. "We're almost afraid to read this passage," suggests Biblical commentator William Barclay, "because to read it seems to be to intrude into the private agony of Jesus."

"When Jesus went to Gethsemane," Barclay continues, "there were just two things he deeply desired. He wanted human fellowship, and he wanted God's fellowship. And as we watched him live out his agony, he met closed doors on both of those desires."

Here he was, in a place we never expected him to be. Alone. Wrestling with God's will. Deeply desiring that his friends, especially his best and closest friends, would stay with him there. But to no avail. "Could you not keep awake for one hour?" he asks of Peter.

The hour had come. It was the hour of our Lord's own despair.

So, we pray. "Where there is despair, let me sow hope."

A few years ago, I helplessly watched as my best friend saw his wife slip deeper, and deeper, then deeper still, into despair. They tried everything that modern medicine seemed to offer: doctors, hospitals, electroshock treatments, powerful psychiatric drugs, hypnosis, talk therapy, wholistic medicine and diet. They prayed. Oh, how they prayed! And others prayed with them and for them. "Father, if it be possible, remove this cup from me," they both prayed. Still, this deep depression refused to release its icy grip.

My friends searched into every person's eyes for some little bit of hope – for something they could hang onto. Just a glimmer, wherever it might be. Something that would take them to another day, without this pain.

Father Albert Haase once wrote, "Hope is an emotion that literally saves us from the present moment we struggle to accept. It gives the nearsighted person who may be fixated on the disappointment or tragedy a pair of glasses that helps them to look beyond—to tomorrow, next month, next year. This far-sighted vision called hope can lift them out of their wintry darkness and wing them into a new dawn. No wonder the poet Emily Dickinson described hope as the 'thing with feathers/that perches in the soul.' "Hope gives the seriously ill the ability to endure painful operations and dream about playing with their grandchildren again. It gives those unjustly imprisoned the strength to see beyond the bars and fight for a retrial. Hope provides the bankrupt the energy to start rebuilding their lives, and gives refugees and exiles the capacity to endure strange customs and keep alive the vision of their homeland. It offers people living in the mindset of war, the prospect of returning to normal lives again." (Haase, "Reflections on the Peace Prayer," p.41)

Yet, sometimes, as it was for my friend and his wife, despair can be so deep, no matter what we say or do, or whatever anyone tries to do. Even hope lies beyond our reach.

Kent Nerburn tells in his book on this prayer about his own encounter with despair while living in a strange land, far from home.

One night, in the distance, in a far street, he heard a strange, muffled sound. He writes, "I looked up and saw a man coming toward me. He was wearing a suit, but his shirt was out and his tie was askew. His gait was unsteady. He lurched and fell against the building as he walked. He was obviously drunk, and sobbing." As the author tells this story, it turns out the man was a well-respected judge in the community. That morning, a young girl had run out in front of his car as he was driving to work. There had been no time to stop. He had struck her, killing her instantly. He had been wandering the streets, drinking ever since.

With his fumbling German, Nerburn explains how he tried to find words that would calm his spirit. But there was no consolation. This judge knew it was not his fault. He knew it was an accident. "I keep seeing her in front of me," he sobbed. "Why could I not stop?"

No matter what Nerburn tried to say, the judge stopped him from speaking. "Don't talk," he said. "I don't need words. I just need to be near somebody."

"I stayed with him," wrote the author, "on that street corner, long into the night. He did not wish to go anywhere. He did not wish to talk. Occasionally, he would take my hand; often he would be overcome with deep and heaving sobs. But whenever I tried to leave or allow him into the privacy of his own grief, he would say, 'NO!' and grab my hand and make me stay."

"That night," the author continues, "I learned something deep about despair and what it means to offer hope. It is the simple gift of our presence that the despairing soul needs, no more, no less."

(Nerburn, "Make Me an Instrument of Your Peace, p. 42)

Sometimes peace makers must become hope for others. That hope can be our simple presence, the gift of another spirit, less overwhelmed with darkness, that refuses to withdraw its light. "Where there is despair, let me sow hope."

Hope is not ours alone to give. It comes from a greater source. Writes the psalmist, "For God alone my soul waits in silence, for my hope is for him. He alone is my rock and salvation, my fortress, I shall not be shaken." (Psalm 62: 5-6)

Even when we can't see it, it is there. Even when our human spirit is too crushed to survive, we know. So, we can sing, "My hope is built on nothing less than Jesus' blood and righteousness." (ELW #596)

◆ ◆ ◆

Let us pray: As you have walked with us in the garden of your own despair, walk with us still, dear Christ, for all this we pray, in Jesus' name. Amen.

Chapter 6

WHERE THERE IS DARKNESS
LET ME SOW LIGHT,
WHERE THERE IS SADNESS JOY

"You are the light of the world. Let your light so shine
before others and give glory to your Father in heaven."
(Matt. 5:14, 16)

Our series continues with two petitions from the "Prayer for Peace." I have combined them because they are really quite similar. Bringing light into a world of darkness and joy into a world of sadness asks each of us to reach deeply into our own needs, as well as into the needs of others.

Light. We long for it in the midst of a Minnesota winter. We longed for it especially in 2020 and 2021, as we faced the international threat of the COVID-19 pandemic. Is there a light at the end of this long tunnel of darkness we wondered? The world had seemed so dark for so long!

Someone once said, "For generations, the story was passed down that fire had been the gift of the sun god. It was a useful gift to the tribe during the day—and a vivid reminder of the sun god's care and concern. The tribal members' daily encounters around the fire reminded them of their relationship to one another and to the sun god."

According to the legend, when the tribe sensed that the rainy season was fast approaching, the elders gathered to select a few members of the tribe to be "Keepers of the Flame." These tribesmen would have the sole responsibility of preserving the sun god's gift during the driving afternoon rains. In this way the fire, and what it symbolized, would be protected during the cold damp days of the rainy season. "If carefully tended, the gift of fire was preserved for another year and another generation." (Albert Haase, "Reflections on the Peace Prayer," p. 47)

What is true about this legend is that light came to be one of the most important symbols in the entire Judeo-Christian tradition. In our scriptural text for today, we hear the words of Jesus as he sends out his disciples to proclaim the coming of the kingdom with the words, "You are the light of the world," charging them to go out and bring light into the darkest corners of the earth. In the first chapter of St. John's Gospel, John takes us back to the beginning of all that is by saying, "In the beginning was the Word, and the Word was with God, and the Word was God. He was in the beginning with God. All things came into being through him, and without him not one thing came into being. What has come into being through him was life, and the life was the light of all people. The light shines in the darkness and the darkness shall not overcome it." (John 1:5)

The writers of our Gospel proclaimed that Jesus Christ was the light. He was, in fact, the true light, John's Gospel proclaims. He is the light which enlightens everyone. Today the "Prayer for Peace" invites you and me to be the "keepers of the flame."

Can we do that? So often it seems that the darkness surrounds everything. As with the ancients in our legend, we are well aware that this is never something we can do on our own. We do it together, with God's help, in the community of the church. Each of us has been entrusted with our own light, and we dare not hide it under a bushel!

Once again, we turn to an illustration from Kent Nerburn, who tells of a moment in his son's school not long ago. His son's teacher, a kind and caring woman, was just packing up to leave for the weekend. Her day had been long, she was tired from a long bout with a chronic and debilitating illness, and she had company coming from out of town. The author had stopped to ask her a question as she hurried to the door. "Down the hall," he said, "we saw a child standing silently. It was one of her students—a young girl from a poor family who always came to school ragged and slightly sad. She followed bravely behind the other girls, but her clothing and her ineffable air of sadness set her apart." (Nerburn, "Make Me an Instrument of Your Peace", p. 52)

As they approached, the teacher waved him on. She stopped and knelt down so she was at the child's level and began talking quietly. Nerburn said that before he left, he turned to see what was happening. The teacher had her hand on the child's shoulder, and they were walking back into the classroom. The little girl was talking animatedly, and the teacher was nodding, as if there were nothing more important as this child and the story she was telling.

My eldest daughter is a teacher. Right now, she is teaching fifth graders during one of the most challenging times in the education of children as the darkness of this virus surrounds us. Nerburn's story made me think of her. It was a simple thing that teacher did. She listened. She shared the touch that everyone is missing in these days of our pandemic. She gave that one last ounce of energy at the end of her day. Bless them, these teachers, who do that every day.

"Where there is darkness, let me sow light." Sometimes, we are too quick to measure our lives by dramatic moments, too ready to minimize the light that we can shine into the small darkness of every day. This beautiful prayer reminds us that we all have light, no matter how faint and fragile. Here is where we can find "shalom." Our prayer reminds us that it is our light that can make a difference, while instilling joy, all at the same time.

✦ ✦ ✦

Let us pray: You have called us, Lord, to be the keepers of the flame. May our lights so shine before others, so that the darkness may never overcome us. In Jesus' name.

Chapter 7

HELP ME NOT SO MUCH
SEEK TO BE CONSOLED, AS TO CONSOLE,
TO BE UNDERSTOOD AS TO UNDERSTAND,
TO BE LOVED, AS TO LOVE.

"A leper came to him, begging him, and kneeling, he said to him, 'If you choose, you can make me clean.' Moved with pity, Jesus stretched out his hand, and touched him, and said to him, 'I do choose. Be made clean!' Immediately the leprosy left him, and he was made clean." (Mark 1:40-42)

"O Divine Master, help me not so much seek to be consoled, as to console, to be understood, as to understand, to be loved, as to love."

Beautiful words from a beautiful prayer, yet so hard to reach, so difficult to model. It's not just the "me generation" that has become myopic. We are, by our very nature as human beings, centered first in ourselves. Today's prayer calls us beyond.

It was just about two years ago that I found myself completely in the hands of God and others, many of whom I had never met before, other than the members of my family, who were waiting in the visitor's area of St. Mary's Hospital in Rochester, Minn. This was the surgical wing. For more than six months, I had been struggling with pain, starting with my lower back, radiating down my leg into my ankle. Pain, that no matter what I had tried to do, refused to go away.

We had packed up early from our winter vacation and come home to Minnesota to see if we could find some answers. After all the exams, the MRIs, the exercises, the therapy, and the consultations by some of the most capable doctors and technicians in the world, it was determined that I would have a laminectomy in an attempt to free up some of those angry nerves that had rendered me almost completely dependent on a walker. It was pain unlike I had ever experienced before.

I had always fancied myself as a little bit of a "road runner," mostly in my own mind. Except for a couple of hips that needed to be replaced, I'd been in good health. But for the past six months or so, I could barely get up in the morning without great pain, pain that it seemed would never go away.

For more than fifty years, I also had been the pastor who came to visit people like me in the hospital. I always had tried to reassure others who were facing similar situations in their lives. This was different. This time it was me who was on the receiving end of things. I was the needy one. I was the one who was afraid. I was the one who was in pain. I found it very hard to think of others, or even to think about God.

So, how could I console when I was the one who needed consoling? How could I understand, when I was the one who needed understanding? How could I love when I was the one who needed love? The shoe was definitely on the other foot, and I didn't like that at all. In addition to the pain, there was a feeling of powerlessness unlike any other I had experienced.

I remember from those days what it meant to me when others stepped into my life with their own consolation, their empathy, their laughter, their looks of deep concern, their love.

My family was there, of course. Or was it "of course"? How could I take their love and their being there with me for granted? My friend and his wife drove all the way down from Duluth on a winter day to be there for me. Joan was there. Our middle daughter, Shelly, stayed the night with me after surgery. She said, before both of us were able to close our eyes that night, "Dad, let's just pretend that we're on a camping trip, and we're in a tent together in the Boundary Waters." We had done this many years before. I could only smile at that wonderful memory we shared. I could only smile at her understanding, her consolation, and her love as I drifted off to sleep in that hospital room, that could have felt so lonely.

The old preacher in the third book of Ecclesiastes once said, "For everything there is a season, a time for everything under the sun." There is a time to be consoled, and time to console. A time to be understood and a time to understand. A time to be loved, and a time to love.

As we pray in this prayer to the Divine Master of our lives, we remember his own selfless surrender and service to others.

They formed the outlines of his footprints in our world that call us to follow him.

I am reminded of the story of St. Francis, the person to whom so many have attributed this "Prayer for Peace." Francis was traveling alone on horseback on the Umbrian Plain when he found himself face to face with a man disfigured by leprosy. Frail himself, and prone to illness, Francis was terrified of the sick man before him, and his first thought was to run and flee.

But he did not. He stepped down from his horse and tentatively walked toward the dying man, put his arms around him, and despite his repulsion, kissed the man's rotting fingers.

He did not do this easily. He did not even do it willingly. If purity of heart had been the measure of his act, it would have had no value at all, for he was filled with abhorrence and nausea at the man who stood before him. But the person in the darkness does not measure your light and does not look upon you as any less if the act you perform is less than pure. What matters is that Francis did it. And in the doing of it, the gift he gave to that leper was exceeded only by the gift he gave to himself".

(Nerburn, p.79)

This latter part of our prayer today gets to the source of what Luther describes as being "little Christs." May you and I be worthy enough to reach out, even to the outer edges of the places it may take us – places we normally would never choose to go. And then, to be grateful for those who have consoled, understood and loved us. No matter what.

◆ ◆ ◆

Let us pray: Thank you, dear Christ, for those who have been "little Christs" in our lives. Thank you for those who have given us a glimpse of you. For there is healing here, when they come. There is peace that comes in Jesus' name. **Amen.**

Chapter 8

FOR IT IS IN GIVING
THAT WE RECEIVE

"He called the crowd with his disciples, and said to them, "If any want to become my followers, let them deny themselves and take up their cross and follow me. For those who want to save their life will lose it, and those who lose their life for my sake, and for the sake of the Gospel will save it." (Mark 8:34-35)

A s we recently watched the made-for-television production of "Jesus Christ Superstar," it became apparent that the words of Jesus were some of the hardest to accept for those who followed him.

"For those who want to save their life will lose it, and those who lose their life for my sake and for the sake of the Gospel will save it." (Mark 8:35)

Taking up our cross and following Jesus is still our biggest challenge in becoming his disciples today. The crowds, and even his disciples, just didn't get it. As we heard "for it is in giving that we receive" from the "Prayer for Peace," we also have wondered how this could possibly be true.

Charles Allen shared with us the story of John Davis from Hiawatha, Kan. There in the Mt. Hope Cemetery there stands a strange group of gravestones.

Allen wrote, "John Davis, a farmer, and self-made man, had them erected. He began as a lowly hired hand, and by sheer determination and frugality he managed to amass a considerable fortune in his lifetime. In the process, however, the farmer did not make many friends. Nor was he close to his wife's family, since they thought she had married beneath her dignity. Embittered, Davis vowed to never leave his in-laws a thin dime.

"When his wife died, Davis erected an elaborate statue in her memory. He hired a sculptor to design a monument which showed both her and him—at opposite ends of a love seat. He was so pleased with the result that he commissioned another statue—this time of himself, kneeling at her grave, placing a wreath upon it. That impressed him so greatly that he planned a third monument, this time of his wife kneeling at his future gravesite, depositing a wreath. He had the sculptor add a pair of wings on her back, since she was no longer alive, giving her the appearance of an angel. One idea led to another until he had spent no less than a quarter million dollars on the monuments to himself and his wife. Whenever someone from the town would suggest he might be interested in a community project (a hospital, a park and swimming pool for the children, a municipal building etc.) the old miser would frown, set his jaw and shout back, 'What's this town ever done for me? I don't owe this town nothing.'

"After using up all his resources on stone statues and selfish pursuits, John Davis died at 92, a grim-faced resident of the poor-house. But as to his monuments, it's strange. Each one is slowly sinking into the Kansas soil, fast becoming victims of time, vandalism and neglect. Monuments of spite. Sad reminders of a self-centered and self-consumed life. There is a certain poetic justice in the fact that within a few years they will be gone.

"Oh, and by the way. Not very many people attended Mr. Davis' funeral. It is reported that only one person seemed genuinely moved by any sense of personal loss. He was Horace Englund, the tombstone salesman." (Charles Allen, "Stories of the Heart," p. 75)

There is so much more to giving that old Mr. Davis just couldn't see. "It is in giving, that we receive."

In his classic book of poetry, Kahlil Gibran writes:

"Then said a rich man, Speak to us of giving.
And he answered:
You give but little when you give of your possessions.
It is when you give of yourself that you truly give."

One of our family's most admired models for giving has always been Joan's mom. For most of her married life, she was a single mom with two daughters. We could never figure out how she could continue to be so generous. She always started with her church, even after her husband died. When her girls were toddlers, she never wavered. She believed in giving 10% of her income first of all to her church. Then it just went on from there to all of the other things that she believed in. Fortunately for us, she believed in her children, even as they grew older and were earning their own income. A check would come in the mail, and she would simply say that the more she gave, the more she had to give. That may not always have been in monetary measurements, to be sure, but it was how she lived her life. It came from her belief in the words of Jesus, when he said, "Those who lose their life for my sake will find it."

The story is told that in the earliest beginnings of the Christian church, a Roman consul called in St. Lawrence the Deacon for a meeting. He said to Lawrence, "The empire right now is in dire financial straits. We need money. You followers of Christ have so many valuable treasures in your churches. I have seen your gold cups and silver candlesticks. I order you to give all the precious treasures of the church to me for the benefit of the empire."

Lawrence surprisingly agreed but said he would need one week to gather them up. The consul approved of the requested delay.

A week later, Lawrence came before the consul again. The consul was surprised that Lawrence was not carrying any bags filled with the church's wealth.

"Where are the treasures?" the consul asked angrily.

"Sir," Lawrence replied, "they are so many that I had to leave them outside. But if you would follow me, I will gladly show them to you."

The consul immediately stood up and eagerly followed Lawrence out of the door. As they walked outside, the consul saw hundreds of poor people, widows, orphans, lepers, the blind, the lame, and the sick. Lawrence made a sweeping motion with his hand and said, "These, sir, are the treasures of our church."

And treasures there are indeed. Once again, our prayer calls us to become, "Little Christs, losing ourselves for the sake of another." If we look carefully, we will see the "Thee beyond the me."

"For it is in giving that we receive."

I grew up in the church having learned a hymn that was really a prayer. We always sang it after the morning offering was received, and it went like this:

"We give thee but thine own, what ere our gift may be.
All that we have is thine alone, a trust, O Lord, from thee."

♦ ♦ ♦

Let us pray: Help us, O God, to be entrusted with the gifts that we have freely received from you. You have given us life, our greatest gift, and you have shown us that it is in our giving that we receive and find ourselves. In Jesus' name. Amen.

Chapter 9

FOR IT IS IN FORGIVING
THAT WE ARE FORGIVEN

"Let anyone among you who is without sin be first to throw a stone at her. And once again, he bent down and wrote on the ground. When they heard it, they went away, one by one, beginning with the elders; and Jesus was left alone with the woman. Jesus straightened up and said to her, 'Woman, where are your accusers? Has no one condemned you?' She said, 'No one sir.' And Jesus said, 'Neither do I condemn you. Go your way, and from now on do not sin again.'" (John 8:3-11)

We continue our series today on our "Prayer for Peace." As a matter of fact, we stand on the edge of the end of this series, and as we do, we hear these words:

"It is in forgiving that we are forgiven."

It's remarkable how this particular petition of our prayer is similar to another petition from a prayer that most of us were taught in the earliest days of Sunday School. I'm referring, of course, to our "Lord's Prayer."

"Forgive us our trespasses," we pray in this prayer, "as we forgive those who trespass against us." The passage of time and teachers has not worn down or lessened the importance of that word "forgive."

When we pray "it is in forgiving that we are forgiven," we would be wise to focus first of all on our need to forgive ourselves.

Author Kent Nerburn observes, "Most people think of forgiveness as something that takes place in the space between two people. And, in many cases, it is. But real forgiveness starts with the self. For until and unless we can forgive ourselves, we can never see the world clearly enough to forgive others. But if we can forgive ourselves, we can allow ourselves the freedom to be less than perfect. We can acknowledge that our shortcomings, and those of others, are but the natural reflections of human beings struggling, by such lights as they have, to do the best they can in this world. We learn to touch the world with a gentler hand." (Nerburn, p. 117)

To pray "forgive us our trespasses as we forgive those who trespass against us" sounds so simple. But it's a very tall order, and it begins very close to home, too close, for many of us to honestly face.

Bryan Stevenson, in his book **"Just Mercy,"** has included a line that I had to read over and over again to gather its full impact. Stevenson is a brilliant and influential lawyer who founded the Equal Justice Initiative, which is dedicated to defending (free of charge) those who often wait on death row after having been unjustly accused and convicted of crimes they hadn't committed. The phrase that the author includes in his book is this: "Each of us is more than the worst thing we've ever done."

It can be so hard, sometimes, to forgive ourselves - to see ourselves as worthwhile human beings who have so much to offer the world, if ever we can allow ourselves to get up off the floor – to live as if we knew we were deeply loved by God. There are lots of reasons for this, including messages that we have heard from significant others all throughout life, that continue to push us back down.

Said Jesus to those who surrounded the adulterous woman, "Let the one who is without sin cast the first stone." And when they heard this, they walked away, leaving her and Jesus alone. "Has no one condemned you," Jesus asked her. "No one, sir," she replied. "Neither do I condemn you," Jesus said. "Go your way, and from now on do not sin again." (John 8:10-11)

Over and over again, Jesus saw the intrinsic worth in others. He sees it in us. "Each of us is more than the worst thing we have ever done." So much more!

In another possibly apocryphal story from the life of St. Francis, a ravenous wolf was terrorizing the countryside around the region of Gubbio, killing all manner of livestock and any humans who happened to be so unfortunate as to have been in his path.

Despite the entreaties of the townsfolk, Francis ventured out to talk to the wolf to get him to change his ways. When he finally confronted the beast, he lectured him soundly.

"Brother Wolf," he said, "I am very sorry to hear about the crimes you commit. You have done dreadful deeds, destroying creatures of God, without mercy. You deserve an awful death, and I understand why the people of Gubbio hate you. But Brother Wolf, I want you to make peace with them so that they need fear you no more and you need not fear them or their dogs. If you do so, I will tell the people to feed you as long as you live, for I know that it is hunger that has driven you in so horrible a fashion."

"The wolf listened intently, and, according to the legend, lifted his paw in a pledge to renounce his murderous ways. He lived out his life as a beloved member of the community, going from door to door for food, and was greatly mourned when he died." (Nerburn, p. 118)

What is important in this story is not its veracity, but the picture of forgiveness, pardon, and reconciliation that it teaches all of us. We each carry a wolf within us and, to a degree, we find it difficult to contain that wolf. Despite our best efforts to keep it under control, it will jump out again and again harming others and often deeply harming ourselves. Those same wolves that live in us also live in those around us, even the members of our own family. They often, even without being aware, will jump out, and seek to damage us and others, by things they say, or do, or fail to say or do.

That's why our church has included the words of confession in our Sunday morning liturgy.

"Most merciful God, we confess that we are captive to sin and cannot free ourselves. We have sinned against you in thought, word and deed, by what we have done, and by what we have left undone. We have not loved you with our whole heart, we have not loved our neighbors as ourselves. For the sake of your Son, Jesus Christ, have mercy on us." (ELW, p.95)

To forgive is never easy. And even when we can, it is hard to forget after the damage has been done. Yet it is forgiveness alone, of all our human actions, that opens up the world to the miracle of infinite possibility. It's as close as any of us can come as human beings to the divine acts of bestowing grace.

◆ ◆ ◆

Let us pray: Our prayer of peace provokes us, O God, to see and understand the wolves that live inside all of us. Help us to forgive, for it is in forgiving that we are forgiven, and it is in doing so that the world may know of your amazing grace. In Jesus' name. Amen.

Chapter 10

FOR IT IS IN DYING,
THAT WE ARE BORN TO ETERNAL LIFE

"And the peace of God, which passes all understanding,
will guard your hearts and your minds in Christ Jesus."
(Philippians 4:7)

In the final words of our "Prayer for Peace," we pray, "For it is in dying that we are born to eternal life." Where is it that we find peace in our troubled world? This beloved prayer would say that it is:

"wherever love is sown, instead of hatred;
wherever pardon has been sown in the face of injury,
wherever faith is planted in the midst of doubt,
wherever hope is given in the midst of despair,
wherever light shines in the midst of darkness,
wherever joy is sown in the midst of sadness."

And in our prayer's concluding words, we build to a grand crescendo as we hear that peace is found:

"in our giving, for it's there that we receive;
in forgiving, for it's there that we're forgiven."
(and at the last)
"in our dying, for it's there that we are born to eternal life."

Look, if you will, our prayer asks of us, into all these places that surround you in your everyday ordinary world, for that's where you'll find peace.

Those of you who have listened to my weekly broadcasts or have gotten to know me as a pastor, know that our family has a cabin tucked away off the beaten track on a beautiful lake. It is the dream of hundreds of Minnesotans. Our cabin has been a gift to us, for more than fifty years. In every season of our lives, we have been blessed with peace there by the shore of Sand Lake in Pine County, Minn.

As I write this, I'm not even sure that we could get there. Our little cabin is no doubt buried in a blanket of snow. But each spring, we know, it's waiting there, to be discovered once again.

Now, mind you, owning a cabin is not just all fun and games. There are, it seems, a never-ending list of chores to be done each year.

We have, for example, a lot of oak trees on our tiny piece of lake shore in the northland. One of the distinct characteristics of some varieties of oak trees is that they can hang onto their leaves all throughout the winter, through some of the wildest winter snowstorms. Why that is we're just not sure. "It's a mystery," says my naturalist friend Jim Gilbert.

But what we do know is that those of us who are lucky enough to enjoy the oak trees on our land also know that as spring advances, those leaves do begin to fall. Finally, as new life oozes through their veins, they give up their will to hang on, making way each year for the life that will follow. What that also means is that we are given the joy of raking some of our leaves in the fall, and then, lo and behold, another batch in the spring. Lucky us!

However, no matter how fiercely those leaves may cling to their branches all throughout the winter, they must eventually let go.

"For it is in dying, that we are born to eternal life."

Sometime ago, I came across a poem that was simply called, "Let Go." It came in a publication from the Courage Center here in Minnesota, and it's sent out to donors and families of people with disabilities. It's too long to include in its entirety, but let me share with you just a few of its lines.

"'To let go' does not mean to stop caring; it means I can't do it for someone else. 'To let go' is not to cut myself off; it's the realization I cannot control another. 'To let go' is to admit powerlessness, which means the outcome is not in my hands.

'To let go' is not to fix, but to be supportive.

'To let go' is not to regret the past, but to grow and live for the future.

'To let go' is to fear less, and love more." (Anonymous)

Just like those oak trees, "letting go" is one of the biggest challenges of our living.

During the COVID-19 pandemic, so many people, in so many aspects of their lives, in so many places on our planet, were asked to "let go" of so many things – things that we all had simply taken for granted. So many others, some of them family, some of them friends, and so many people that we never even knew were asked to "let go" so that others could live. I, for one, am so grateful for each and every person who faithfully wore a mask, who socially distanced, and who got vaccines. I give God thanks for those who gave up their freedoms, and in some cases even their livelihoods, knowing that it was going to take all of us to make it through. Yet, we had to say goodbye to way too many all around the globe. But thank God for all those who were mindful that only as we join together can we play a part in savings others. Blessed be those who lost their lives in the midst of it all, for they are truly with the angels now in heaven and on earth.

Thank you, God, for those who were able to trust and believe, that "it is in dying, that we are born to eternal life."

In the hymn "All Creatures of our God and King," the words of which have been attributed to St. Francis of Assisi, the final verse goes like this:

"*And you most gentle sister death,*
Waiting to hush our final breath,
Alleluia, Alleluia!
Since Christ our light has pierced your gloom,
Fair is the night, that leads us home.
Alleluia, Alleluia."
(EBW - #835)

Ultimately, here is our peace. Here is God's shalom. Praise him.

• • •

Let us pray: We are eternally gratefully, O God, for your giving us the Lord of life and death that we have known in Jesus. Help us to let go of our fears; fear less, love more, and let your peace come into our hearts. Amen.

SECTION 2
SAINTS AND SINNERS

The only thing necessary for the triumph of evil is for good people to do nothing. (Edmund Burke)

The tragedy of life is not death, but what we let die inside us while we are living. (Norman Cousins)

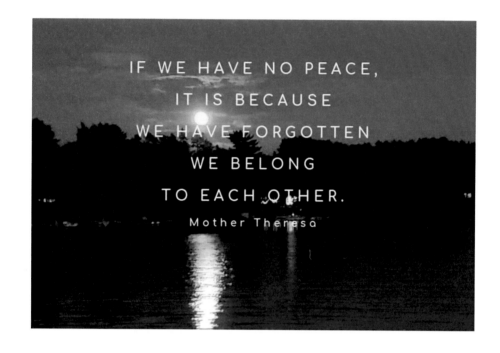

IF WE HAVE NO PEACE,
IT IS BECAUSE
WE HAVE FORGOTTEN
WE BELONG
TO EACH OTHER.
Mother Theresa

Chapter 11

DIETRICH BONHOEFFER:
CHILD OF GOD, GIANT AMONG MEN

*"Why are you cast down, O my soul? And why are you
disquieted with me? Hope in God; for I shall again praise
him, My help and my God." (Psalm 42:1,2,5)*

From time to time, I have chosen to accent some of the
"Lesser Festivals and Commemorations" of our church.
These special days often feature special events and people
in the church's history, and I have included them in this section
called "Saints and Sinners." They are noted in our Lutheran Book
of Worship, pages 15-17, and each has played a very special role
in guiding us in our search for peace in a troubled world.

On April 9, we focused our attention on one of those giants
of our church history, Dietrich Bonhoeffer. On that day, he was
executed for his participation in an attempt to assassinate Adolf
Hitler in 1945.

For Bonhoeffer, his resistance to Nazism was an act of obedience to Jesus Christ. As someone once put it, "His life and death and writings throb with the simple downright faith of one who has met Jesus Christ and accepted the ultimate consequences of that encounter in the world."

In 1933, Hitler and the National Socialist Party came to power. As both a student and a pastor, young Bonhoeffer recognized that there was a subtle shift from respecting the office of the chancellor of his country to worshipping the man who held the office. Bonhoeffer also recognized and resisted the growing anti-Semitism in his country and was appointed by the Confessing Church to organize and head an illegal clandestine seminary for the training of pastors in Pomerania.

Most of you know the rest of the story. He and others could no longer stand idly by while Hitler sought to reach his ultimate dream of taking over the world. He and other church leaders began to speak out. He was arrested and convicted of treason. He was sentenced to wait out his death at the concentration camp in Buchenwald. While there, as a pastor, he was given permission to minister to the sick and dying among his fellow prisoners. Many of them, like himself, were facing their final hours. Every week in 1943 and 1944, ten or twenty others were sentenced to death by a military court. His ability to comfort the anxious and depressed prisoners around him became legendary. To many around him, he stood like a giant among men.

But that was only one side of the man. The other side was one who lived and loved this world. He, a giant among men, was also but a child of God. Even in his own mind he became a riddle unto himself. One day, he gave expression to this conflict in his soul in a moving poem entitled "Who am I?" written in his prison cell.

Who am I? They often tell me
I stepped from my cell's confinement
Calmly, cheerfully, firmly,
Like a squire from his country house.

Who am I? They often tell me
I used to speak to my warders
Freely and friendly and clearly,
As though it were mine to command.
Who am I? They also tell me
I bore the days of misfortune
Equably, smiling, proudly,
Like one accustomed to win.

Am I then really all that which other men tell of
Or am I only what I myself know of myself?
Restless, and longing and sick, like a bird in a cage,
Struggling for breath, as though hands
Were compressing my throat,
Yearning for colors, for flowers, for the voices of bird,
Thirsting for words of kindness, for neighborliness,
Tossing in expectation of great events,
Powerlessly trembling for friends at an infinite distance,
Weary and empty at praying, at thinking, at making,
Faint and ready to say farewell to it all.

Who am I? This or the other?

Am I one person today and tomorrow another?
Am I both at once? A hypocrite before others,
And before myself a contemptibly woebegone weakling?
Or is something within me still like a beaten army,
Fleeing in disorder from victory already achieved?
Who am I? They mock me these lonely questions of mine.
Whoever I am, Thou knowest, O God, I am thine. (The Cost of Discipleship-p.18-19)

Born on February 4, 1906, Bonhoeffer was executed by special order at the concentration camp in Flossenberg, just a few days before it was liberated by the Allies. For his willingness to stand up against the man who had become one of the most feared in the world, he shall always be remembered. His faith was in Jesus Christ, and him alone.

Those who attended his memorial service in London on July 27,1945, felt that something had happened in Germany that could not be measured by human standards. They felt that God himself had intervened in the most terrible struggle the world had witnessed so far by sacrificing one of his most faithful and courageous sons to expiate the crimes of a diabolical regime and to revive the spirit in which the civilization of Europe has to be rebuilt.

We close our thoughts today with a portion of the poem that Bonhoeffer himself wrote on New Year's Day, 1945, just days before his execution:

◆ ◆ ◆

Let us pray: "When now the silence deepens for our hearken-ing. Grant we may hear thy children's voices raise. From all the unseen world around us darkening. Their universal pain, in thy praise."
(Bonhoeffer-p. 21)

Grant us faith, dear Christ, always to know that whomever we are, we are Thine. Amen.

Chapter 12
JOHN ROBERT LEWIS
A GOOD KIND OF TROUBLE

"But how are they to call on one whom they have not believed? And how are they to believe in one whom they have never heard? And how are they to proclaim him, unless they are sent? As it is written, 'How beautiful are the feet of those who bring good news?'"
(Romans 10:14-15)

Having hosted weekly radio broadcasts for a long, long time, I have a couple of regrets. Sometimes I feel them more deeply than I do at other times. But because of my own schedule and the church's schedule, I often had to write and record my broadcasts ahead of time.

Then, something happened in the world that I wish I could have addressed. A hurricane hit the coast. A man was killed in the streets of our city. An injustice had been done to a person or persons. Or, something wonderful happened that filled our hearts with hope. But because my words had already been moved forward, toward the air waves, it seemed too late for me to try to empathize, or sympathize, or whatever the case might be.

That happened in August of last year with the funeral of Congressman **John Robert Lewis**. Though John Lewis is not listed in our church's list of special saints, I could easily lobby for his name to be included in any future lists. I watched part of that three-hour funeral just after I had written my weekly broadcast. I must confess that before the funeral, I really had known so very little about this great man. When he was growing up, his mother always cautioned him not to get into trouble. But despite his mother's wishes, he decided that he must. And so, he chose to get into what he called "good trouble."

There are some remarkable parallels between Congressman John Robert Lewis and the apostle Paul. They both chose to get into a "good" kind of trouble. All that came about because they wanted people to know the great good news of Jesus Christ. Listen again to the words of our text today: "But how are they to call upon one in whom they have not believed? And how are they to believe in one of whom they have never heard? And how are they to proclaim him unless they are sent? As it is written, 'How beautiful are the feet of those who bring good news?'"

Both the great apostle and John Lewis believed they had been sent. They literally gave everything they had to let that message of good news be heard. It was a message of sacrifice, a message of kindness, and a message of freedom against all odds. It's a message for all people. It's my prayer that we can still hear it today. Remember how we used to sing about it in Sunday School?

We sang, "Jesus loves the little children. All the children of the world. Red and yellow, black and white, they are precious in his sight. Jesus loves the little children of the world." They are *all* precious in his sight. And so are we! Pretty simple message really. But so hard for us to believe.

In his final words, shortly before he died of pancreatic cancer, John Robert Lewis addressed our nation one more time. In his address, he quoted the great Dr. Martin Luther King Jr., whom he had heard on the radio as a young man. It was King who was talking about the philosophy and discipline of non-violence. He said that we are all complicit when we tolerate injustice. He said it is not enough to say it will get better day by day. He said each of us has a moral obligation to stand up and speak out. "When you see something is wrong, you must do something," he said.

"Though I may not be with you," said Lewis as his physical condition worsened," I urge you to answer the highest calling in your heart and stand up for what you believe. In my life, I have done all I can to demonstrate the way of peace, that the way of love and non-violence is the more excellent way. Now, it is your turn to let freedom ring."

Writes Frederick Beuchner, "What is both Good and New about the Good News is the mad insistence that Jesus lives on among us, not just as another haunting memory, but as the outlandish, holy and invisible power of God working not just through the sacraments, but in countless hidden ways to make even people like us, loving and whole, beyond anything we could possibly pull off by ourselves." (Wishful Thinking, p. 33)

In closing, let me share with you a prayer by **Pastor Ted Loder**. He called it, "Sometimes it Just Seems Too Much."

Sometimes. Lord,
It just seems to be too much:
  too much violence, too much fear;
  too much of demands and problems;
  too much of broken dreams and broken lives;
 too much of war and slums, and dying;
 too much of greed and squishy fatness
   and the sounds of people
    devouring each other.
 and the earth;
 too much of stale routines and quarrels,
  unpaid bills and dead ends;
 too much of words lobbed in to explode
  and leaving shredded hearts and lacerated souls;
 too much of turned away backs and yellow silence,
  red rage and the bitter taste of ashes in my mouth.
Sometimes the very air seems scorched,
 by threats and rejection and decay
   until there is nothing
    but to inhale the pain
    and exhale confusion.

Too much of darkness, Lord,
 too much of cruelty
   and selfishness
    and indifference...

Too much, Lord,
 too much,
   too bloody,
   bruising,
   brainwashing much.

Or is it too little?
*   too little of compassion*
too little of courage,
* of daring,*
*   of persistence,*
*   of sacrifice;*

too little of music,
*   and laughter*
*   and celebration?*

O God,
make of me some nourishment
*   for these starved times,*
some food for my brothers and sisters,
* who are hungry for gladness and hope,*
that, being bread for them,
* I may also be fed*
* and be full. Amen.* (Guerrillas of Grace, Prayers for the Battle)

♦   ♦   ♦

Let us pray: "Walk with the wind, brothers and sisters, and let the spirit of peace and the power of everlasting love be your guide." Amen. (John Robert Lewis)

Chapter 13

FLORENCE NIGHINGALE & CLARA MAAS
TWO REMARKABLE WOMEN

"Whoever welcomes you, welcomes me, and whoever welcomes me welcomes the One who sent me. And whoever gives even a cup of cold water to one of these little ones in the name of a disciple—truly I tell you, none of these will lose their reward." (Matt. 10:40-42)

W
hile I have called Dietrich Bonhoeffer a giant among men," we now hear the story of two that we might easily call giants among women."

We continue to honor these remarkable models of our Christian faith on the day of their death, August 13, in that same section of our hymnal that has been named "Lesser Festivals and Commemorations" of the church. (ELW, p 15-17)

Let me begin by sharing a description of one of these women that appeared in the "London Times" in the mid-1880s. See if you can guess which of our two remarkable women this may be.

"She is a ministering angel, without any exaggeration in these hospitals. And as her slender form glides quietly along each corridor, every poor fellow's face softens with gratitude at the sight of her. When all the Medical Officers had retired for the night and silence has settled down upon the miles of prostrate sick, she may be viewed alone, with a lamp in her hand, making her solitary rounds."

Sounds like a great question for a television quiz show like "Jeopardy," don't you think? Her name is **Florence Nightingale**, and we honor this remarkable woman on the day of her death in1910.

It was said that she was "stubborn, opinionated, and forthright." But she had to be to accomplish all that she did. She lived to be 90 years old, a testimony to just how stubborn she was.

The other of these two women is **Clara Maas,** a woman who was given an entirely different lot in life, and who died in the year 1901 at the tender age of 25. Both will be remembered in our church as "renewers of society."

In some ways, these two "giants among women" could not have been more different.

While Florence Nightingale came from a well-connected British family of wealth, Clara Maas came from an impoverished family in a very devout Lutheran home in East Orange, N.J.

Clara Maas was the oldest of 10 children and entered nurses training at the age of 19. She worked for many years without any income of her own, volunteering to serve without pay in both the 7th and 8th Army Corp in Cuba and later in the Philippines. For most of her young life, she was glad to be given only room and board in compensation for her work.

It was her death in 1901 that roused public sentiment to put an end to the Yellow Fever experiments that were done on human beings in order to find a cure for that dread disease during the Spanish American War. Clara Maas volunteered not once, but twice, and risked her life to serve as a nurse in that war. Having contracted Yellow Fever the first time, and surviving, she volunteered once more. The second time, the disease took her life. It was thought that because she survived the first time, she would have an immunity that would prevent her from becoming ill. Unfortunately, that was not the case. She died an early death. She received $100 for each time she volunteered, the equivalent of $3,000 today

Florence Nightingale responded to her call to serve during the Crimean War in Turkey. It was her emphasis on the importance of sanitation and clean water, both in her nursing practice and in her books of nursing, something that we now take for granted, that dramatically changed the possibilities for survival in those who had been injured. Thanks to her efforts in changing that entire culture of care, the mortality rate among those who were injured during that war decreased dramatically.

Interestingly, Florence Nightingale also had a Lutheran connection, having visited the Lutheran religious community in Kaiserwerth, Germany, where she witnessed Pastor Theodor Fliedner and the deaconesses working with the sick and depraved. That experience was a turning point in her life, and she wrote her first book about nursing following that profound experience.

On the 100th anniversary of her death, Clara Maas was pictured on a 13-cent U.S. postage stamp commemorating her service to others. Florence Nightingale was one of the few women ever to receive the "Order of Merit" from the British government. It was she who inspired the poetry of Henry Wadsworth Longfellow when he wrote:

Lo! In the houses of mercy
A lady with a lamp I see
Pass through the glimmering gloom,
And flit from room to room.

So, we honor two giants among women on August 13. Each made dramatic improvements in the health care of others, and we continue to honor nurses all over the world, especially now, as we struggle with the devastation of our recent pandemic. Both women and men are still bringing healing to others, through their tireless efforts and their loving care, while at the same time risking their own lives for the sake of others.

♦ ♦ ♦

Let us pray: O God, your Son came among us to serve, and not to be served, and to give his life for the life of the world. Lead us by his love to serve all those to whom the world offers no comfort and little help. Along with these two remarkable women we highlight today, may we too be inspired to bring hope to the hopeless, love to the unloved, and peace to our troubled world. For it is in Jesus' name that we pray. Amen.

Chapter 14

TOYOHIKO KAGAWA:
A FORGOTTEN PROPHET OF PEACE?

"Then they came to Capernaum, and when he was in the house, he asked them, 'What were you arguing about along the way?' But they were silent, for on the way they had argued with one another about who was the greatest. He sat down and called the twelve and said to them, 'Whoever wants to be first must be last of all and servant of all.'" (Mark 9:33-35)

Those words of Jesus from St. Mark's Gospel have not been easy to follow for most of us. One of those that our church remembers who struggled with those words was **Toyohiko Kagawa.** We honor him on the day of his death, April 23, 1960.

Among the "Lesser Festivals and Commemorations" listed in our hymnal (p.15), Toyohiko Kagawa has been called "A

Renewer of Society." Chances are you may never have heard of him.

In many ways, he was more diligent in his search for peace in our troubled world than anyone else we have considered thus far.

He was born in 1888, the son of a philandering business man and his concubine. At the age of four, he lost both of his parents. From that rather austere and fragile beginning, he was sent away to a school where he learned from two American missionaries and teachers, Dr. Henry M. Meyers and Charles A. Logan, both of whom had their roots in the Southern Presbyterian Church of the United States of America. After taking Toyohiko under their wings, they converted him to Christianity and baptized him at the Tokushima Church in Japan. His conversion was a radical departure from the major religions of his Asian roots, and he was ultimately disinherited from his other family connections in Japan.

As he began to study and learn more about his new found faith, Toyohiko was troubled by what he saw to be the students and seminarians in the college and seminary he attended be more concerned with the technicalities of doctrine than with the lifestyle that they lived. He came to believe that Christianity in action was the truth behind all the doctrines of the faith. It was his conviction that, first and foremost, the parable of the Good Samaritan was the heart of what it meant to follow Christ. So that he himself not only "talked the talk" of the faith, but also "walked the walk," he took the bold step at a young age of moving into a slum in Kobe, Japan. He decided that it was his calling to serve the poor. To do so, he must live as they lived. There, in a shed six-foot square, he served others as a missionary, social worker and sociologist for several years. As a result of that experience, he published "Research in the Psychology of the Poor," a study of the poor that proved to be a great awakening for many in his own country, revealing practices of illicit prostitution, informal marriages and the practices of accepting money to care for children and then later killing them. He went even further, taking part in labor activities in 1921 and 1923 in an effort to lift his people beyond the squalid conditions of poverty. He was arrested, not once but twice, for his participation. After his release from prison, he helped organize relief efforts in Tokyo after the Great Kanto Earthquake in 1923.

He wrote more than 150 books, was nominated for the Nobel Prize in literature in 1947 and 1948, and for the Nobel Peace prize in 1954. When he came to the United States, he soon became almost a household name, and his following grew wherever he traveled. Everything he wrote seemed to focus on the betterment of society, flowing from the heart of his own convictions of his Christian faith.

So why have some called him the forgotten prophet of peace? Why is his name so seldom mentioned among the so-called "giants of the Christian faith?" It has been suggested by some that much of his "fall from grace" and personal popularity among Christian leaders had to do with the second World War. He was foremost an advocate for peace in all that he did and wrote, but his name and nationality could only be associated with that terrible war, which left such an ugly scar on everyone who was affected.

Even though after the war he literally threw himself into leading the charge for the reconstruction of his nation and became one of the foremost advocates for Japanese democracy, his own popularity faded. Despite his heartfelt promotion for world peace in all that he did, his halo had been tarnished for his association with all of atrocities of the war that he had continued to oppose. We, too, here in the United States, have had our own "halos tarnished" as we look at our role in how our own citizens were treated in our own country during that same war, simply because of their cultural and national origins. War does that. Fear and hate lead the way. Pray for peace. Work for peace. Search for it in any way that you can.

◆ ◆ ◆

Let us pray: You have called us to live our faith, dear God, but so often we fall so short of the vision you have shown us in your Son. Help us to remember that our message of faith is a message of the Kingdom of God, centered in a message of love and peace. In Jesus' name. Amen.

Chapter 15
KATHARINA von BORA
THE POWER BEHIND THE THRONE

"Love is patient; love is kind; love is not envious or boastful or arrogant or rude. It does not insist on its own way; it is not irritable or resentful; it does not rejoice in wrong doing, but rejoices in the truth. It bears all things, believes all things, hopes all things, endures all things. Love never ends. And now faith, hope and love abide, and the greatest of these is love." (I Corinthians 13:4-8, 13)

I have chosen this beautiful and familiar passage of St. Paul's 13th chapter of 1st Corinthians because it really is a love story that I want to tell you about. Though it isn't very likely that the two people I want to tell you about were actually in love when they were first married, they grew together into a story that most of us would agree became a strong and lasting love right up until their death.

This is the story of the marriage of a Roman Catholic priest and a nun. **Katharina von Bora** and **Martin Luther** each in their own way played a central role in the Reformation of the Christian church on earth.

In this chapter we will center our attention on Katharina. Her husband, Martin Luther, sometimes referred to her as "Dear Kate." In our church, we commemorate the life of Katharina von Bora on December 20, the day she died in 1552 at the age of 53.

If one were to search the pages of the history of the Reformation, one would find there was very little written about Katharina. That's probably not too surprising, since she lived in a day and age when women were plain and simply given very little regard. I hope that we have now begun to see how wrong this has been in so many ways.

Much of what we know about Katherina von Bora has actually come to us from the writings of Martin Luther himself. Despite that, many would now regard Katharina as one who helped define Protestant family life, and as one who set the platform for the marriage of the clergy.

Though some of the facts about her early life are not clear, what we do know is that she came from a family of some means, and that her father sent her at the tender age of five to study at a Benedictine cloister in 1504. At the age of nine, she was moved to the Cistercian monastery in Nimbschen, Germany, where her maternal aunt was already a member of that community. After several years of religious life, she grew dissatisfied with life in the convent. It wasn't long after that she became fascinated with the growing reform movement that was swirling around the church spearheaded by Martin Luther himself. Ultimately, she conspired with several other nuns to flee in secrecy, and she contacted Martin to ask for his help.

On Easter Eve, April 4, Luther sent Leonhard Koppe, a city council man of Torgau and also a merchant who regularly delivered herring to the convent, to assist in the nun's escape. She and several other nuns piled into Koppe's covered wagon among the fish barrels and fled to Wittenberg where Luther taught. It was there that each of the nuns sought to begin a different life.

When Luther agreed to help the nuns in their great escape, he first asked their parents and relatives to admit them again into their homes. They declined to receive them, however, believing that to do so would make them accomplices to a crime under the canon law of the church.

According to other historical sources, Luther was soon able to arrange homes, employment, or marriages for each of them who had chosen to leave the convent. Katharina, we are told, had a number of suitors. She told one of Luther's friends, however, that she would only be willing to marry Luther himself or his friend, Nicholas von Amsdorf. Phillip Melanchthon, one of Luther's closest friends, was shocked that Luther would even consider marrying due to the potential scandal that could severely damage the entire Reformation movement.

Interestingly, Luther's father encouraged him to marry. After pondering his future for some time, Luther ultimately decided that his marriage would "please his father, rile the Pope, cause the angels to laugh, and the devils to weep." On June 13, 1525, a 42-year-old monk and a 26-year-old nun were joined in holy matrimony.

They grew to respect and honor each other. She became known as a clever administrator, managing the household, bearing six children, and organizing the family finances. Their home was in Luther Stadt, the former Augustinian monastery where Luther had lived before the Reformation began. She was able to grow much of what they ate in her own private garden. She raised livestock, cooked and brewed her own beer. Luther even went so far as to allow her to deal with his publishers in all that he had written. In something totally unheard of at that time, he made her his sole heir.

After his death in 1546, she wrote, "He gave so much of himself in service not only to one town or country, but to the whole world. Yes, my sorrow is so deep that no words can express my heartbreak, and it is human impossible to understand what state of mind and spirit I am in...I can neither eat nor drink nor even sleep. God knows that when I think of having lost him, I can neither talk, nor write, in all my suffering." (Wikipedia sources – Katharina von Bora)

I close with Martin Luther's own quote: "There is no more lovely, friendly, and charming relationship, communion or company, than a good marriage." Martin Luther was by no means the first cleric of his time to marry. His prominence and his position set the tone for much of Christianity when it came to norms of clergy being married.

◆　◆　◆

Let us pray: Thank you dear Lord, for Katharina von Bora, for her love for the great reformer of the Christian church, and a woman who has helped us in our own understanding of marriage and the family. Thank you always for your love, dear God, which sees each of us through the tough times, and the love which you have promised will never end. Amen.

Chapter 16

THE CARTHUSIANS AND TERESA OF AVILA: MONASTICS IN OUR MIDST

"Rejoice in the Lord always—again I will say rejoice. Let your gentleness be known to everyone. The Lord is near. Do not worry about anything, but in everything by prayer and supplication with thanksgiving let your requests be made known to God. And the peace of God, which passes all understanding, will guard your hearts and minds in Christ Jesus." (Philippians 4:4-7)

One of the things I enjoyed in my weekly radio broadcasts was exploring the contributions of some of these special saints and sinners in our church's history. Today, I would like to take you back to another. Her name is **Teresa of Avila.**

On page 16 of our hymnal, Teresa is called a "teacher and a renewer of the church." We honor her on the date of her death on October 15, 1582.

So many of these influential figures that we have considered thus far seem to have come to us from long ago. In many cases, we've been taken back to horse and buggy days. But even our recent saints and sinners have never heard of computers, or Facebook, to say nothing of tweeting and texting, terminology that has now become such a common part of our everyday vocabulary. At the same time, each were very human beings, struggling to make sense of their world the same way we are trying to make sense of our own. Each of us, saints and sinners alike, are trying to find our way, and looking to our faith in God to help us.

Are you aware that we have our modern-day mystics and monks?

Here in Minnesota, for example, not far from the city of St. Cloud, we have St. John's Abbey, where presently there are 133 professed monks who have given themselves entirely to God.

A few years ago, my friend **David,** an attorney from Vermont, began to tell us about a monastery near his home town. There are a group of monks who have devoted themselves to a rigorous life of work and prayer, and have become an isolated community separated from the rest of the world. They are the **Carthusians.** There aren't very many of them. In fact, this particular Carthusian community is the only one in the United States. When they enter the community, they pledge themselves to a lifetime of seeing or speaking to no one outside of their cell, except once a week, when they are given the chance to interact with their "brothers" for a short time.

A few years ago, when Joan and I learned that one of our daughters had been diagnosed with cancer, David asked if we would like to have the Carthusians pray for her. It was then that we learned of the miracles that have been attributed to their community and to their life of prayer.

One of those miracles came about when a very wealthy business man who had heard of their community asked the leader if the Carthusians would pray for his family member who had been also diagnosed with cancer. When all the medical and scientific attempts to save this person had been exhausted, the monks began to pray. She recovered. In gratitude, the wealthy business man donated a beautiful 7000-square-mile piece of land on Mount Equinox in Vermont so that they could build their monastery and continue their ministry here in the United States. Our friend, David, who at one point had his own sights on the priesthood, is their one intermediary who lives outside their community. He keeps contact, gives legal advice, and communicates through their leader with the outside world.

When Joan and I said, "Yes" that we would very much like to have our daughter included in their daily prayers, David seemed pleased, and so were we. **Brother Mary James** who communicates with David, to this day asks how our daughter is doing. I think he takes special pride knowing that the Carthusians are even reaching out to a Lutheran pastor and his family!

You should know that our daughter, Kristina, is now six years out from her diagnosis and is cancer free. We are grateful and give thanks for their prayers, as well as the prayers of the many others who know and love her, and the incredible medical support of the Mayo Clinic here in Minnesota.

But I digress. Let's go back to our 16th century mystic, Teresa of Avila.

Teresa lived in Avila, a city just 50 miles west of Madrid, Spain. Writes **William White** in his book, **"Speaking in Stories,"** "Anyone who can combine discipline and celebration, prayer and dancing, and a sense of reform with a sense of humor is a person worthy of attention. Such a woman was Teresa, a 16th century mystic and master of the one liner." (p.89)

She entered a Carmelite convent in her home town, but it seems as though entering a convent at that time was not really much of a retreat from the rest of the world. Life in a convent was pretty much a reflection of the permissive attitudes of the rest of society. Prayer was largely ignored. Teresa soon learned that the spiritual needs she longed for were not being satisfied. She began to dream of a reform movement based on a rigorous life of both work and prayer, much like the modern Carthusian "brothers" with which we began this chapter. It was her deep desire to step away from the affluence that was found in most of the orders of her day, and give her life a brand-new focus centered in Christ.

Her order began with just three nuns. They chose to live their lives in almost perpetual silence, again like the Carthusians mentioned earlier. She was a woman who was not to be deterred. Having experienced resistance to their ideas, Teresa went directly to Rome and eventually secured permission from the Pope to begin her convent in the disciplined manner she was seeking. That couldn't have been an easy journey in those days, crossing the mountains on foot into France, then Italy, from Avila all the way to Rome.

What I found refreshing about her monastic movement was the joy that she insisted be a part of those who bonded together. Music and dancing were a regular part of convent life. She once wrote "virtue and merriment go hand in hand. Just because the 'order' is austere," she said, "there is no need for austere people."

It seems that others who were seeking a new life felt the same. For soon the order was flourishing. In all, she founded 32 convents and almost singlehandedly began a movement that swept Spain. Though she could certainly be described as a mystic and was frequently led to ecstasy and rapture, she was somehow able to keep her contemplative life in balance. "Contemplation and action are never to be separated," she mused. "Just as an active life is barren without contemplation, so the contemplative life is empty without action."

In her writings, it is not hard to discover her quick wit and sense of humor. "Lord, save us from sullen saints," seemed to be at the heart of who she was. Even her conversations with God were filled with wit and charm. Once she confided to God that, "If I had my way, that woman wouldn't be the Mother Superior." God answered, "If I had my way, she wouldn't be either."

Another time when Teresa was attempting to cross a stream, she slipped off her donkey and fell headlong into the water, nearly drowning. It is reported that God reminded her that he chastises those he loves. "I treat all my friends that way," he said. Teresa apparently turned her eyes heavenward and sputtered, "No wonder you have so few friends, when you treat the ones, you have so badly." (White p. 91)

I think it's fair to say that we need a reformer in our world today who will remind us that there is a season for everything.

There is a time for seriousness, and a time for laughter. We have lots of room in our own spiritual practices to discover a sense of holiness, without losing our sense of humor, and our sense of mission. We could use another Teresa in our midst.

♦ ♦ ♦

Let us pray: Thank you, dear God, for those who inspire us to grow closer to you. Thank you for the "monastics" in our midst, even today, sometimes without our even being aware. Send them, send us, into the world around us, we pray in Jesus' name. Amen.

Chapter 17

MARTIN RINKART
POKING AROUND FOR SIGNS OF HOPE

"I will not leave you orphaned. I am coming to you. In a little while the world will no longer see me, but you will see me; because I live you also will live. On that day you will know that I am in the Father; and you in me; and I in you." (John 14:18-20)

W hat a great promise Jesus leaves with us today! "I will not leave you orphaned; I am coming to you." In his April 8, 2020, weekly column in the Christian Century, editor-in-chief Pastor Peter Marty wrote the following: "We typically use the term 'natural resource' to refer to things like water, forests, and land deposits containing minerals and fossil fuels. We could make a compelling argument, however, for an even more precious natural resource; human relationship. I am convinced that love and social connections matter more than anything else in life."

Marty goes on to say that we are living in a time when these precious natural resources of human relationships become even more valuable than ever. That's just one thing we have learned from COVID-19.

What each of us has learned through all of this is how much we have missed that incredible natural resource that we had taken for granted for most of our lives--the connection with others in our day-to-day living. Night after night, we watched and experienced those poignant scenes and pictures of sadness; families standing outside the windows of nursing homes or extended care facilities, peering in, trying to see someone they love, staying outside for fear of spreading the dreaded virus. Loneliness, helplessness, isolation and uncertainty, have caused so many of us to poke around for signs of hope.

So hard, for so many! My heart aches for those who wait on both sides of the glass. Yet, even in the midst of that same isolation, most of us agreed that to open our world too quickly would only make the situation worse.

Reflects one writer, "lost profits and limited liberty or unlimited suffering and lost lives?" Neither of those two options would be an easy choice.

In that same article in the Christian Century mentioned above, Peter Marty reminds us of a person that I first encountered as I wrote the story behind one of our most beloved hymns. The hymn is "**Now Thank we All our God.**" The author is **Martin Rinkart.**

Early in Rinkart's lifetime, he was a gifted musician in several prominent churches in Saxony, Germany. He later became an ordained pastor to the people of Eilenberg and served in that capacity for thirty years before his death. Those years coincided almost exactly with the dreadful thirty-year war that continued in that part of the world. The city of Eilenberg, because it was a walled city, became a magnet for refugees during the war. It did not take long for famine and pestilence to take hold. In 1637 alone, 8,000 people died of disease. Those included were Rinkart's own wife, other clergy, and most of the town council. He alone was left to minister to the entire city. He preached at burial services for as many as 200 in one week. Being the faithful and caring pastor that he was, he gave away everything he owned, except for the barest essentials, in order to care for his community.

In the midst of the incredible communal suffering that surrounded him, Rinkart wrote a hymn with words that have since become familiar to most of us.

Now thank we all our God, with hearts and hands and voices.
Who wondrous things has done, in whom this world rejoices.
Keep us all in grace, and guide us when perplexed.
And free us from all ill, in this world and the next. (LBW, #839)

It's a hymn that's worth coming back to as we deal with the perils of our own lives, such as the one we continue to battle right now as the variants of COVID take on a life of their own, and as we wait to be reunited with our most precious human resources.

In life and in death, we *can* give thanks, knowing that in Christ, God will never leave us or forsake us as we live out these days.

★ ★ ★

Let us pray: For those who have literally given up their own lives caring for others, dear Lord, we are thankful. For the Martin Rinkarts in our history and our world, we are eternally grateful. Lead us always through the days of our uncertainty, when we do not know where we are going, and assure us of your grace, as you have promised. In Jesus' name. Amen.

Chapter 18

HARRIET TUBMAN
AND THE TRUTH SHALL MAKE YOU FREE

"Then Jesus said to the Jews who had believed in him, 'If you continue in my word, you are truly my disciples, and the truth will make you free.'" (John 8:31-32)

In the long list of names that our church commemorates, there is at least one who has become the embodiment of Jesus' words in the 8ᵗʰ chapter of the Gospel of John more than any of the others, **Harriet Tubman.**

Said Jesus, "If you continue in my word, you are truly my disciples, and the truth will make you free."

March 10, the date of her death, has been named "Harriet Tubman Day."

If some would have their way, she would be the person looking back at you every time you reach into your billfold seeking to pull out a $20 bill. Though it hasn't happened yet, in 2016 the United States Treasury announced that Harriet Tubman's image will replace that of former President Andrew Jackson on the $20 bill. Many, including myself, are hoping that will happen soon.

Let me sketch for you a brief history of Harriet Tubman's life.

She was born in 1822 in slavery on a plantation in Dorchester County, Md. When she was born, her parents, Harriet ("Rit") Green and Benjamin Ross, named her Araminta Ross. They called her Minty.

Harriet's mother worked as a cook in the plantation's "Big House." Benjamin was a timber worker. Harriet had eight brothers and sisters, but the realities of slavery eventually forced many of them apart, despite Rit's attempts to keep the family together. When Harriet was five years old, she was rented out as a nursemaid, and she was whipped when the baby cried, leaving her with permanent emotional and physical scars.

Around age seven, Harriet was rented out to a planter to set muskrat traps and later rented out as a field hand. She later said she preferred physical plantation work to indoor domestic chores.

It became apparent at a very early age that Harriet had a deep desire for justice, for herself, and for her people. When at the age of 12 she spotted an overseer about to throw a heavy weight at a fugitive slave, Harriet stepped between the slave and the overseer. The weight struck her head. She said later about the incident, "The weight broke my skull—they carried me to the house all bleeding and fainting. I had no place to lie down on at all, and they laid me on the seat of the loom, and I stayed there all day and the next." Her "good deed" left her with headaches and narcolepsy for the rest of her life, causing her to fall into a deep sleep at random. She also started having vivid dreams and hallucinations, which she often claimed were religious visions. Her infirmity made her unattractive to potential slave buyers and renters.

As I learned about this period of history when I was growing up, I was somehow given the impression that folks who lived in slavery were happy people, positive people, who had the "joy of Jesus" in their hearts, and who sat around campfires at night and sang "Kum ba yah" roasting marshmallows all the while.

Nothing could have been further from the truth. Through the years, as their history has become more and more transparent, we have learned the true stories of the brutalities and horrors that African American slaves faced each and every day of their lives. "The truth shall make you free," said Jesus.

On September 17, 1849, Harriet and her two brothers, Ben and Henry, escaped their Maryland plantation. Though her brothers were frightened for their lives and changed their minds, Harriet persevered, and with the help of the so called "Underground Railroad," traveled 90 miles north to Pennsylvania and to freedom.

When she finally reached the north, she said later that she looked at her hands to see if she was the same person now that she was free. She said there was such a glory over everything that the sun came like gold through the trees, and she felt she was in heaven.

Here is where her real story actually began, and why she is remembered today.

At the time, most people wouldn't have known Harriet Tubman by her given name, because it wasn't long before she became known as "Moses." That was her code name for the

"Underground Railroad," in which she soon became an influential "conductor" for much of her life before the Civil War. The "Underground Railroad" was a term designated to a network of secret routes and safehouses established in the United States during the early to mid-19th century, used by African American slaves to assist in their escape into free states and Canada.

Harriet Tubman has been credited with making 19 return trips to the South, daily risking her own life, helping deliver at least 300 fellow slaves primarily into Canada. She boasted, "I never lost a passenger." Through her guidance of so many to freedom, it wasn't hard to see how she earned that nickname of "Moses."

So, of all the people who have risked their lives for freedom, why have we in the church chosen to honor this one woman on March 10 by naming a day in her honor?

Perhaps this quote will clarify.

In the midst of her courageous acts and threats to her life, she once said, "I always tole God, I'm going to hold stiddy on you and you've got to see me through."

Her friends, her fellow abolitionists, claimed that the source of Harriet Tubman's strength came from her faith that God was the deliverer of the poor and the weak. She stands in the train of some of the most significant prophets of the Bible. To once again quote our scripture for today, "She continued in (his) word; she was truly his disciple," and the truth, Harriet Tubman knew, "would make her free."

She once said she "would listen carefully to the voice of God as she led slaves north, and she would only go where she felt God was leading her." Fellow abolitionist Thomas Garret once said of her, "I never met any person of any color who had more confidence in the word of God."

Her favorite hymn, which she loved to sing in her deep contralto voice, was "Swing Low, Sweet Chariot." She was an active member of the African Methodist Episcopal Church in Auburn, NY, where she settled in her later years. You can visit her home even today.

The last words she uttered (according to her obituary in the "Auburn Citizen") were ones of faith. "I go to prepare a place for you." She died in 1913. She was truly our modern-day Moses, and she lived to be 93 years old.

◆　◆　◆

Let us pray: Once again we thank you, O God, for all those who listen to your voice, as you lead us to work for justice and freedom in our world. May we also learn to speak your truth in love, so that others may know what it's like to be free. We pray in Jesus' name. Amen.

SECTION 3
REFLECTIONS
THROUGH THE YEAR

"For everything there is a season, and time
for every matter under heaven."
Ecclesiastes 3:1

Note from the author: Almost all of the reflections in this section were written during the year (2020-21) when the COVID 19 pandemic began to consume our lives and our world, and the days that followed. When this book went to press, new variants continued to threaten us, dominating the daily news, and our conversation. My writings during this time and my radio broadcasts were also focused on finding meaning and hope in the midst of what we were all experiencing, wondering where God might be leading us in our search for peace, and what we might learn from these incredibly challenging times.

Chapter 19

THE STORY OF THE RED ENVELOPE
ADVENT AND CHRISTMAS

"For unto us a child is born, unto us, a Son is given."
(Is. 9:6)

I've told a lot of stories in the many years of hosting our church's weekly radio broadcast. Perhaps the most memorable one for me, and I know for our family, was first told on Faith Alive on Christmas Day in 2005.

It was called "The Red Envelope," and it was written by Nancy Rue. I found it in a little book called "Christmas in My Soul." The story became a favorite in our family, mainly because it developed into a wonderful tradition that each of us has loved. The story began like this:

"Tom was gone. How could I possibly face Christmas without him? Worse yet, the children were acting as if it was Christmas as usual. How could they?"

It's told in the first person. As we listen, we quickly learn that the author's husband, Tom, had suddenly died the year before, shortly after Christmas. She had always made a big deal about Christmas, and her family loved all the little things that she did each year to make it a memorable and festive holiday. When Tom was alive, he had always chided her, telling her she over did at Christmastime. He complained about how commercialized the holiday had become. "You've gone hog wild again," he would always tell her, and then each year he would add his one generous contribution. He would spend months looking for the right worthy cause. Instead of buying a gift for her and the children, he would write a check in her name to them, be it the Muscular Dystrophy Association or a local church that needed a new roof. He would put the check in a red envelope and tuck it onto a branch of their Christmas tree. "This'll last all year," he'd tell them. "Maybe even change someone's life."

This year was different. Now that Tom was gone, she just couldn't get her heart into Christmas.

Slice. Scoop. Plop.
I don't feel like doing this.
Slice. Scoop. Plop.
I don't want to do this. I don't want to shop.
Slice. Scoop. Plop.
I don't want to decorate. I just want to skip it.
Slice. Scoop. Plop.
And pretend I didn't notice this year.

After the last of the ready-made cookie dough was in the oven, which was a far cry from the bejeweled affairs she'd baked for 26 years, she tried desperately to muster up the energy to do some Christmas shopping for the children.

"Ken was right," she thought to herself as she made her way through the crowds at the mall. "This is all a joke." It really was everything he hated—canned music droning its false merriment somewhere in the nebulous background—garish signs, luring her to buy—squabbling tired-looking families, dragging themselves around, worrying about their credit card limits as they snapped at their children. It had never bothered her before, but this year was different.

The story is delightfully told, and it all comes to a climax on Christmas morning after she hit an all-time low the day before. She is certain that the kids aren't even thinking about their dad being gone this year, and they have simply gone on with their lives. She hadn't forgotten at all. The last thing she did on Christmas Eve after all the kids had gathered back at home and gone to bed, was to place a red envelope on the tree with a check enclosed for "The American Heart Association." She ached with the emptiness inside of her.

In the morning, as she tried to shake the sleep from her eyes, she heard her one grandson cry out, "Come see, Grandma. Come see all these red things."

What she saw first was her family, perched on a couch like a row of "deliciously guilty canaries." What she saw next was the family Christmas tree, dotted with bright red envelopes. As she opened each one, her eyes overflowed with tears.

Not only had her children not forgotten, but each one had placed their own red envelope on the tree sometime during the night, without saying a word to anyone.

From Paul was a check for Big Brothers, for kids who have to grow up without their dad. From Amy, to the church, where she best remembered her father-in-law. From Ginger, for the Committee to Aid Abused Women," because Dad always treated you like a queen." From Ben, a $20 bill for a local drug program for kids, "since Dad was all freaked out about me staying clean."

The last envelope was lumpy and jingled. "That's from me, Grandma," Danny said, little bow-mouth pursed importantly. "For lost dogs—you know, like that one me and Grandpa rescued."

"You know what's weird," one of the children finally exclaimed. "I feel like Daddy's right here with us." They clinked their coffee and cocoa mugs together and drank a toast, each with tears streaming down their faces." ("Christmas in My Soul" (vol. 3), Joe Wheeler, Doubleday 2002)

End of story. But maybe not. At least not in our family.

After that story was read for the first time at our Christmas gathering that year, and before we began opening any other gifts, that same tradition became a part of own family tradition and has continued to be ever since.

The very first red envelope in 2005 was a gift given to "The Smile Train" from Joan and me to provide surgery for children who were born with a cleft lip and palate.

Now, each year after the reading of the story, even before we search for the nut in the rice pudding, the recipient of that year's gift is announced. And you know what's even better? A few years ago, unbeknownst to us, our adult daughters got together and presented a very generous red envelope gift of their own. It was given to children from struggling homes in the St. Paul area, providing clothing items, toys, and a gift certificate for each one. That year there were two red envelopes on our tree and have been every year after.

Now this year? 2020? Because of the pandemic, we gathered around a fire pit in the backyard of our oldest daughter's home. After the presentations of the two red envelopes, we were suddenly blown away when our oldest granddaughter, Emily, suddenly "discovered" another red envelope, hidden behind one of the pine trees in their yard. When they handed it to me, the words on the outside of the envelope said, "It's our turn." That's when I began to blubber again.

All eight of our grandchildren had pooled their money, more than $500, and provided a beautiful gift for people in need, through a program that Emily researched called "Project for Pride in Living," designed to help young people get on their feet and break out of poverty. It was a gift that will never be forgotten. Each of our grandchildren's significant others, those who have them, were also part of the gift this year!

"This is the best part of our family Christmas celebration each year!" they would be quick to say.

♦   ♦   ♦

Let us pray: Gracious and giving God, center our thoughts and hearts on the joy of giving to others. And thank you for giving to us the greatest gift of all in the birth of our Savior. We pray in his name, Jesus Christ our Lord. Amen.

Chapter 20

ADVENT REFLECTIONS

The winds blow sharply through the pines.
Earth like iron, buried in snow.
Embers glow, in my darkened room
Late on a deep winter's night.

The eyes of God peer down this night,
As they wait for a star to be born.

Cold and old are the eyes this night,
Weary and waiting and tired.

Through thick, thick, lenses,
God stares down hard,
And waits for a star to be born.

There! On the windswept plains near Bethlehem!
Where a woman and man wend their way!

They come to a place where the winds take their rest,
While the world is holding its breath.

The old, cold eyes, fill with tears tonight.
Long for the peace
promised for years.

Chapter 21

A CHILD IN OUR LIVES
(Christmas)

Gently...
You've caressed our world
   With warmth and wonder.

You have seen us through the rocky times,
   You have urged us on.

You caused the fragile roots of roses
   To know the nurturing
   Of a deep
   Abiding love.

Each year we grow--
   And wistfully become
   A people less afraid to risk.

We know that you are there
    Dying by our side
    Yet resurrecting always,

Faithful people
    To a place of new beginnings.

Let it be, dear Lord. Let it be.

Gently...
    You've caressed our world
    With warmth and wonder.
    From unsuspecting places.

Sinful, smelly, stables,
Bethlehem's
    Emmanuel.

God with us--
    Evermore!
(Terry R. Morehouse, Christmas 1985)

Chapter 22

IN THE DAZZLING GRACE
BAPTISM OF JESUS

"But now, thus says the Lord, he who created you, O Jacob, he who formed you, O Israel. I have called you by name. When you pass through the waters, I will be with you, and through the rivers they shall not overwhelm you; when you walk through fire you shall not be burned, and the flames shall not consume you. For I am the Lord your God, the Holy One of Israel, your Savior." (Isaiah 43:1-4)

One of my favorite people died at Christmas time. Her name was Shirley Huskins, and her family chose this portion of scripture to be read at her funeral.

I've always loved this reading from Isaiah. If anyone has any doubt that there is gospel in the Old Testament, I would advise them to re-read the book of Isaiah. The prophet's poetic words are addressed to the nation of Israel as they near the end of their exile in Babylonia, assuring them that despite the way things seem to be right now, and even in spite of their wayward past, God's faithfulness is never-ending. His love for his people is eternal.

Speaking on behalf of God, as prophets often do, he tells God's people, "Do not fear, for I have redeemed you; I have called you by name."

Each year, shortly after Christmas, we in the church observe a Sunday that we call, "The Baptism of our Lord." It's not by accident that Isaiah's words have been chosen to be read on that Sunday to lead us in our readings of Scripture. Not only are we reminded of God's reassuring words to his beloved Son, Jesus, on this day, but we are also reminded of the words that were heard in our own baptisms, which for many of us were a long, long time ago.

"Do not fear," the prophet reminds us. "For I have redeemed you. I have called you by name." Terry Morehouse, child of God, you have been sealed by the Holy Spirit, and marked with the Cross of Christ, forever.

Make no mistake. That's good news! But is it also true that God protects us as this Scripture suggests? Is it true that when we "pass through the waters," they shall not overwhelm us? That "when we walk through the fires, we shall not be consumed?" Tell that to the people in California, or Oregon, or Australia, or Colorado who most recently have had those words tested in their own lives. If we were not consumed, they must wonder, then why did it hurt so much to lose everything? If the rivers did not overwhelm us in our recent hurricanes, then why did it feel as if we were being swallowed up? Does God protect us from these things? Tell that to those who have lost a dear one to death while everyone else is enjoying the holiday season!

In a July 2007 edition of the Christian Century magazine, Scott Bader-Saye faces that question head on when he tells of a friend named Steve, who was dying of cancer. Steve received a well-intentioned, but hurtful, letter from a woman who suggested that if "he had more faith," God might yet *heal* him. "Far from providing comfort," Scott said, "the letter struck Steve like a hot iron of judgment."

With the help of his twin brother—for he was by then too weak to take a pen in hand himself—Steve drafted a reply that read in part:

"I share your faith in the power of God to heal and sustain us. There may be times, though, when God's great miracle is not the miracle of physical healing, but the miracle of giving us strength in the face of suffering."

"As I read the Bible," Steve continues, "God promises to remove all suffering in the next life, though not necessarily this one. In this world, we will sometimes weep, suffer and die. But in the New Jerusalem, 'God shall wipe away all tears from their eyes, and there shall be no more death, neither sorrow, nor crying, neither shall there be any more pain, for the former things have passed away.' (Rev. 21:3-4) I sincerely hope that if my cancer continues to grow, no one will see it as a failure of my faith, even if I died when I am still young. I do not claim to know God's will, but I do know that I am in God's hands, whether in life or death."

Thank you, Steve, for sharing your faith with us. For that is our promise too, fellow travelers.

Even though it may seem as though we are burned beyond the recognition of ourselves, or swallowed up in the midst of floods that sweep into our lives, God is with us. God's love—the bridge that carries us into the future – the place "where there will be no more sorrow, a place where God will wipe away all tears from our eyes." (Rev. 21:4:)

Writes the great preacher William Sloane Coffin, reflecting on the sudden death of his own son, "So I shall, and so let us all, seek consolation in that love which never dies, and finds peace in the dazzling grace that always is." (A Chorus of Witnesses, p. 266)

◆ ◆ ◆

Let us pray: "Hold Thou thy cross before my closing eyes. Shine through the gloom, dear Lord, and point me to the skies. When the waters rage and the fires roar, around us, and within us, may we always find peace in the dazzling grace that is." In Jesus' name. Amen.

Chapter 23

SUMMON US TO YOUR LIGHT

In our prayer for the third Sunday in Epiphany we pray: Lord God, your loving kindness always goes before us and follows after us. Summon us to your light, and direct our steps in the ways of goodness that come through the cross of your Son, Jesus Christ, our Savior and Lord. Amen.

"Summon us to your light," we pray. We could easily say this is the message of the entire season of Epiphany.

It's been called "The Season of Light." In St. Matthew's Gospel, those who were called left the darkness to follow Jesus. This season begins with a star that came to rest over Bethlehem – a star that led the Magi from the east to search for him.

It is said that stars, angels and dreams are all a piece of the same reality – that they are all messages from God, shreds of glory loose on earth, invitations to the closeness of divinity.

Megan McKenna in her "Stories and Reflections for the Sunday Readings" reminds us of why these messages, these interruptions, are needed at specific junctures in God's plan in a story she calls "The Hidden Star."

"Once upon a time there was a gathering of stars, a shining convergence of light. They came together to boast of their service to humanity and what they had done in obedience to God's command to shine forth and bring light in the heavens. They knew that their glory lay in serving those he had put upon earth. They didn't gather very often, but when they did, it was a sight to behold.

"They shimmered and shone, pulsed and throbbed, with every color of white; they left off tiny specks of light and brilliant showers, bursts, and long lingering trails. One star spoke amid the music of their coming together. 'I am the pole star," she sang out. "If it weren't for me, humans would be lost. They would have no sense of direction, no feel for distances. Their journeys would be nightmares that never ended. Because of me, they know where they are on the earth and can go from one to the next.'

"Another star spoke and said, 'Well, I don't have a name, but what I have done is really spectacular, for I am the star that proved Einstein's theory of relativity correct. Yes! That was me! I darted behind the sun at just the right moment during an eclipse and forever changed the shape of earth's science.'

"The others beamed and glowed in recognition. Others spoke up and cited their contributions to science, to art, and to music, to the beauty of earth's dome. The music and sound spilled over and over and wove in and out of the light. Then everyone heard a small cough, and stopped for a moment. It was the sun, who politely but firmly pointed out that he, too, was a star, probably the most potent and necessary for the service he rendered daily to the creatures and dwellers on the earth. The stars all deferred to the sun's obvious power.

Then someone noticed one star who hadn't said a thing. It was quiet and remote, and it looked like it was trying not to be noticed or even seen. It was singled out and asked what it had done for humankind. It was silent for a moment, and then confessed honestly that it hadn't done a thing. In fact, it hadn't even been discovered; its existence was totally unknown.

After a moment of silence, some of the stars exploded with laughter and derision, commenting, 'Of what use is a star if it isn't known to exist?' After all, they were told to be lights in the firmament and to shine forth to the glory of God and to encourage human kind!

After a long period of silence, the hidden star spoke again. 'So, my contribution is really very crucial, you see, for I keep those who search the heavens awake! I remind them of mystery, of the unknown, and what has yet to be discovered. In fact, I think my being so hidden lures them further and further into the skies, and to the awe and grandeur of God who is maker and keeper of all things in the heavens, and I'm glad you have challenged me, for now I know that I want to stay hidden for a long time. I want those who search the heavens to know they have much yet to discover and that there is so much mystery out there. Perhaps they will remember that the heavens reflect much below and that the mystery within them is just as deep and far flung among themselves.

The stars were silent as they listened. All returned to their places in the sky, humbler and more in awe of God's hidden plans and secrets. For now, even they wondered what they didn't yet know about themselves, and about the Creator who is the light itself." (Advent, Christmas, and Epiphany, Megan McKenna, p. 223-224.)

◆   ◆   ◆

Let us pray: Hidden stars, secret plans, quiet mysteries, a loving kindness, a world of peace. These are the promises of Epiphany. So great are the mysteries! So many that we still can't find. We wonder at these great mysteries, O Lord, and wait for them to be revealed. Summon us into your light, O God, and direct our steps to the way of peace. In Jesus' name. Amen.

Chapter 24

WHEN THE WHOLE WORLD
SEEMS TO BE UNRAVELING

"He first found his brother Simon, and said to him, 'We have found the Messiah!'" (John 1:41)

Each year, during the season of Epiphany in our church year, we are invited into the earliest days of Jesus' ministry and into the lives of his first disciples. "We have found the Messiah," Andrew excitedly proclaims to his brother Simon Peter. And forever after their lives were changed.

There is something about Jesus, the Gospel writers want us to know, that is unlike any other. There is something about Jesus, they believed, that if you see it, your life can never be quite the same again.

What about for us? There is something about Jesus that may excite us, annoy us, intrigue us, make us angry or happy, yet for many, once he has touched our life, it's almost impossible to ignore him.

That's because Jesus invites us to look into the mystery of God in a brand-new way. Even when God alludes you, you can still find Jesus, inviting you back to faith again.

Not long ago, I picked up Betty Smith's classic novel about growing up in the Williamsburg slums of Brooklyn from 1902-1919. "A Tree Grows in Brooklyn" is a wonderful story that focuses on the Nolan family, whose daughter Francie and son Neeley knew more than their fair share of the privations and sufferings that are the lot of the city's poor.

When their father died of acute alcoholism at the age of 35, young Francie and Neeley are trying to process his death. After holding back the tears for a long time, both of them turned into a dark side street in their neighborhood and sat on the edge of the walk with their feet in the gutter...and wept. That continued for a long time, there in the cold street. At last, when they could cry no more, they talked:

"Neeley, why did Papa have to die?" Francie asked her brother.

"I guess God wanted him to die," her brother responded.

"Why?"

"Maybe to punish him."

"Punish him for what?"

"I don't know," said Neeley miserably.

"Do you believe God put Papa in this world?"

"Yes."

"Then he wanted him to live, didn't he?"

"I guess so."

Deep in her troubled young mind, Francie struggled, trying to make some sense of why her father had to die at such a young age. If God truly wanted to punish him, she wondered, what good is it? In her mind, her papa, whom she dearly loved, was dead. If God was so great, if God knew everything and could do anything, why didn't he help Papa, she thought, instead of punishing him like her brother had said?

"Maybe you shouldn't talk about God like that," said Neeley apprehensively.

"If God has charge of all the world," said Francie, "and the sun and the moon and the stars and all the birds and trees and flowers and all the animals and people, you'd think He'd be too busy and too important—wouldn't you—to spend so much time punishing one man—one man like Papa?"

"I don't think you should talk about God like that," said Neeley uneasily. "He might strike you down dead."

"Then let him!" cried Francie fiercely. "Let him strike me down dead right here in the gutter where I sit!"

In their grieving, these two young siblings waited fearfully. Nothing happened. When Francie spoke again, she was quieter.

"I believe in the Lord, Jesus Christ, and his mother, Holy Mary," Francie finally said. "Jesus was a living baby once. He went barefoot like we do in the summer. I saw a picture where he was a boy, and had no shoes on. And when he was a man, he went fishing, like Papa did once. And they could hurt him, too, like they couldn't hurt God. Jesus wouldn't go around punishing people. He knew about people. So, I will always believe in Jesus Christ."

They made the sign of the cross as Catholics do when mentioning Jesus' name. Then she put her hand on Neeley's knee and spoke in a whisper.

"Neeley, I wouldn't tell anybody but you, but I don't believe in God anymore."

"I want to go home," said Neeley shivering. (Betty Smith, "A Tree Grows in Brooklyn")

My guess is that almost every one of us has had thoughts like Francie's cross their minds. But like Neeley, we find them pretty scary to talk about and choose to leave them deep inside.

When the whole world seems to be unraveling, when we enter the loss of some one that we love, when nations and cities and tiny towns are struck by random acts of violence, when evil people and mentally unstable people go on a rampage at a grocery store or in a school, when we just feel lost—when any kind of peace seems far away, it's hard to figure out where God comes in. We, too, wonder why God isn't trying to do something about the way we're feeling. We wonder what God is all about.

But there is something about Jesus that invites us to look again.

It's true that there are a lot of things about Jesus we don't understand either. But if we choose to follow him, he can lead us through our questions, so that someday we may find the answers.

· · ·

Let us pray: So many questions, and so few answers, Lord. In all these times, give us Jesus. Lead us to see him there on the shores of our lives, or in the center. In the midst of our tears, we find the human side of God that we long so desperately to know. Trust him to see us through, especially when our world is unraveling. We pray in his name. Amen.

Chapter 25

SOME EVENING THOUGHTS
IN EARLY SPRING

Sitting here—
    In a place I've often been.
    My favorite view…here on Cherrywood Lane.
    Looking out, over the trees, that we have watched,
Some of them since infancy. (Theirs not mine)

Limbs dancing, even in the waning winter winds---
Still quietly welcoming, to all who see.

The grass is barren,
Waiting for warmth to seep into its pores.

And so…the leaves are gone, except for just one tree,
My favorite,
The towering Black Hills Spruce.

Aging issues, stalk my body and my mind,
Continued pain.
Yet, I'm still very much alive.
Thankfully.
Through all these years.
Brushed with grace,
instilled with peace,
In the early evening light.

(Terry R. Morehouse, April 2, 2020)

Chapter 26

PLANTING SEEDS OF GRACE

"And other seeds fell on good soil and brought forth grain, some a hundred-fold, some sixty, some thirty. Let anyone with ears listen." (Matt. 13:9)

Some time ago, in the pages of one of my other books, I told you about my friend Ben. As a matter of fact, I told you that my friend Ben has a problem.

He's a gambler. Oh, not the kind of gambler that first might come to your mind, who sits around in smoky rooms, a cigar and drink in hand. Nor will you find my friend in the local casino, playing blackjack or cranking the handle of a slot machine. That's not the kind of gambling that he does.

No. Ben is a farmer. Or at least I should say, he has been one for most of his life. He actually retired at the end of this year's harvest. He also was a teacher and a coach in that small town near his family's farm near Amboy, Minn., just a little south and west of Mankato.

Every year, it seemed, was different than the year before. As you know, farmers often have to gamble on the weather. Often, they never know from year to year or day to day what the weather's going to bring.

Some years there's a drought. Other years there's hail or too much rain or not enough. You never knew. But every once in a while, for him like last year, there is a wonderful balance of sunshine and showers. You could see Ben smiling from 'ear to ear' (so to speak) as he looked out and saw those soy beans and those stalks of corn waving in the wind, plump, and calling out to him with the promise of the best year ever.

Every time I hear this parable read from the gospels, it makes me think of Ben. This image of the one who is sowing seed, has been around, it seems, forever.

Sowing seeds, writes Pastor David Miller, also seems to capture a truth about our lives. "In every moment of every day, our words and actions sow seeds of one kind or another, into the lives of others," he said. "And the soil of *our* lives receives the seeds that others cast our way." (Sundays and Seasons 2020, p. 207)

Some of them grow, and some of them not so well. Think about that, if you will. Parents and grandparents plant seeds of goodness and grace into the lives of their children, hoping they will grow into responsible and happy adults. Teachers sow seeds into the lives of their students. Even preachers are in the business of sowing seeds into the lives of those who will listen.

Every Sunday School teacher and confirmation teacher sows seed, often wondering, does it make a difference? Will the seeds take root and grow in the souls of those children? Will the children know how precious they are to us and to God, and how much love they have to give to others?

Pastor Miller says he wondered about that a lot at a recent service of prayer he attended. Here is how he describes it:

"Seventy motorcyclists and friends gathered around two deep gashes in the turf where one of their number crashed trying to escape the police. He was gravely injured, and disabled for life. I was invited to reflect with them and lead prayers. In other words, I was there to sow seeds of hope and God's compassion. It was a joy that also surprised me, exposing my assumptions and my lack of faith," he wrote, "but I soon saw the shoots of God's kingdom, sprouting in the lives of the most heavily tattooed congregation I have ever served. Someone, somewhere, had been sowing seeds in their lives long before I showed up. Seeds of compassion had taken root in them, or else they would not have been there."

As he describes that day and that experience, he remembers how under a summer sun and the watchful eyes of the local police, a communion of care appeared, as they hugged, signed a huge card, and humbled their heads in prayer, their invulnerability having been stripped away to reveal their humanity beneath their black leather jackets.

The pastor whispered a silent "thank you" into that Sunday circle. Thank you to all who had planted seeds of grace in their lives. Thank you to those who planted deeds of faith in *his* heart that he had the eyes to see the beauty of that moment. Thank you to the profligate sower who gleefully cast seeds of the kingdom into the tail winds of Harley Davidsons.

"You just never know," wrote Pastor Miller, "where the seed of God's loving kingdom will find receptive soil. Sometimes it happens in the least likely place, say, like our lives." (Sundays and Seasons 2020, p. 208)

"Listen!" said Jesus, "if you have ears." God's seed seeks to root deeply in your heart and grow into something truly alive and beautiful.

And so for today, be thankful – thankful for every person and moment that sowed this seed in *your* heart.

And sow some seed yourself! Go ahead. Be a gambler like my friend Ben. Be generous and throw seed everywhere. Remember. You have the "master gardener" on your side. You just never know where the seed will grow.

♦ ♦ ♦

Let us pray: Almighty God, Your Word is cast like seed into the ground. Now, let the dews of heaven descend, so that abundant fruit may grow. So, when the precious seed is sown, life-giving grace bestow, that all whose souls the truth receive, its saving power may know." Amen. (LBW, #516)

Chapter 27

WAITING FOR WORMS

The icy grip of winter's clutching fist
Refuses to relent.
What happened to the spring?

Forsooth forsythia! Thou can'ts not—not yet
Alas O blossoms of the peach! Hold back sweet smell!

I remember when in Minnesota's days of other winters,
No one dared to claim they saw a robin.
These days, too early for the earthworm on the sidewalk.

Yet still we waited—
Then as now.
Yet still we hoped,
Then as now.

Could life be sending us another test of our endurance?

But, we will wait again upon the freshness of the promise.
When tenderly once more our Creator God unravels.

Buds to leaves again,
Trees to green again,
These hopes of new beginnings.

Even us.

Chapter 28

THANKS FOR THE RAIN

For the blessings of the rain, O Lord.
That gently fell.
Soaking deep, stretching out the bogs,
    The marshes,
    The rivers and the lakes
    Of our beloved state
We give you thanks.

For giving hope to farmers,
Happy hearts to those who putter in their yards,
    Soft and gentle smiles
    To garden growers everywhere.
For all these gifts,
We give you thanks.

For giving bathtubs to robins,
Bursting buds to lily pads,

The sap of life to trees and bushes
And oh…so many other things,
We lift our hearts in thanks and praise.

When it comes to the rain, O Lord,
There will always
Be someone to complain.
But I'll pray for their pain, and say,
"Thanks for the rain!" Amen.

Chapter 29

A PRAYER FOR SPRING

For the early morning bird-song,
That cheers my waking day.
For the leaping-green of daffodils,
   Who anxiously await their favorite time of year.
For buds, that burst, their chests outstretched,
   Seeking the warmth of April's sun.
O God, Creator Lord, and King,
   I give you thanks and praise.

For now, the northward flight,
   Of ducks, and geese against the azure blue.
For lakes once locked, now free, their waves unleashed,
   To play, in the season's rushing breeze.
For the busy muskrat, building at the water's edge,
   The noisy caws of crows, disturbing quiet waters,
O God, Creator Lord, and King,
   I give you thanks and praise.

For the sprigs of hope that bubble up within me,
The deep-down freshness of my walk at dawn.
For each of nature's signs that point to You,
Give thanks to You, O Christ, and underscore,
The promise of your never-ending Love

With all of these there comes an even greater sign,
A Cross, a victory, an Easter…In my life forever.
O God, Creator Lord, and Savior,
I lift my heart in thankfulness and praise. Amen.

Chapter 30

UNLIKE ANY OTHER DAY
(Palm Sunday)

"Let the same mind be in you that was in Christ Jesus, who though he was in the form of God did not count equality with God a thing to be grasped. But emptied himself, taking the form of a slave, being born in human likeness. And being found in human form, he humbled himself, and became obedient to the point of death—even death on a Cross." (Philippians 2:5-8)

The ancient hymn from St. Paul's letter to the little church at Philippi sets the stage for yet another Palm Sunday in our lives.

Little did we know that Palm Sunday 2020 was to be a day unlike any other that we've known. As we look back, it was almost "spooky."

One of the options for the "Prayer for the Day" on Palm Sunday asks, "that we might share in Christ's obedience."

Little did we know then how challenging that could be for us! Obedience, as one commentator put it, "not as adherence to a command, or rule, but as the fruit of trust in God's goodness, justice, and vindication." Our scriptures remind us that God can be trusted with our lives. Obedience flows from God's trustworthiness.

Trusting God with our lives is not so easy, as we know. One can't help but think of how different Palm Sunday 2020 was from all the others we have known. Memories of gathering near the back of the sanctuary along with all the choirs, and especially the little ones, all decked out in their white robes with red bow ties. Parent volunteers scurrying about trying to keep order amidst the chaos, while Johnny is swatting Susie with his palm branch and Susie is howling for her mom. Then the timpani begins its steady beat, the trumpets and the organ begin to play "All Glory Laud and Honor," everyone begins to wave their palms and excitement fills the air. On all those "other" Palm Sundays, the church was filled to overflowing. In 2020, the doors were locked. The sanctuaries were empty. We sat at home and watched online, observing social distancing, a phrase that most of us had never heard before. It was now a part of every conversation.

It really was a day unlike any other that we've known. No children at all. Only in our homes and memories. No palm branches. No triumphant trumpets leading us down the aisle. No public worship anywhere! So different! Yet still we had our memories.

And still we prayed: "By your spirit, keep us in the joyful procession of those who with their tongues confess Jesus Christ as Lord, and with their lives praise him as their Savior, who lives and reigns with you and the Holy Spirit, one God, world without end." Amen. (ELW-p. 29)

So, we asked ourselves, what *could* we do on a day like this one?

Well, we knew we still could pray, as we listened in our homes or on our radios, as our church and pastors still reached out to us with this triumphant message that would remain the same.

St. Paul and others invited us once again to look at our lives, giving thanks for the God in whom we CAN place our trust, maybe and most especially on a day like that. We still could give thanks for those who were working tirelessly to keep us safe from this silent enemy that threatened us. Give thanks--for those who were working 24/7 to save the lives of those among us struggling to survive while risking their own in the effort. Give thanks--for those working around the clock to find a vaccine that would promise hope for all of us.

We discovered on that day and those that followed that there WAS something we could do even when our churches were empty. We could let "the same mind be in us that was in Christ Jesus, who emptied himself, and became obedient unto death, even death on a cross." (Philippians 2: 5-8)

Even as we sat in the quiet of our homes, we could quietly sing, "Jesus keep me near the cross, there's a precious fountain; free to all, a healing stream, flows from Calvary's mountain."

For, you see, on *this* Palm Sunday, his story became our own once more. Clearly, we could see the road that lay before him and know that he walked that road for us. Ultimately, it doesn't matter that our churches were silent, because he takes us there with him, to the foot of the cross. For he is our only real hope, even when the world as we know it has been turned upside down, on a day that was unlike any other day we've known.

The pews of our churches may have been empty, but still our hearts were full.

◆ ◆ ◆

Let us pray: Preserve us in these troubling times O Christ, knowing that because of you, our hearts can still be full, even when our pews are empty. In his name we pray. Amen.

Chapter 31

PLENTY? OR NOTHING?
(Easter)

"So, they left the tomb quickly with fear and great joy, and ran to tell his disciples. Suddenly, Jesus met them and said, 'Greetings!'" (Matt. 28:8-9)

A biblical commentator I read recently wrote, "Easter is a tough Sunday to preach, because everyone knows how the story ends. Christ is risen! Christ is risen indeed!"

What could one possibly add to that?

"Well," writes Paul Hoffman, "depending on one's state of mind, one might answer, 'Nothing' or 'Plenty.'"

He goes on to say, "The Bible urges us toward the latter. There is plenty to say. Not because we don't know how the story ends, but because we don't know just where it will catch us, and what we will be in the middle of when it does." (Sundays and Seasons, Year A, 2020)

Where *does* Easter catch you?

Life is complicated. When the women came to the tomb on that first Easter expecting to find death, they found life instead. Just as we had no idea that when we awakened on Easter morning 2020, we would be surrounded by death, as the statistics of those dying from COVID-19 continued to mount, day after day. Life *is* complicated that way. The story of our lives and the Biblical story of Jesus is filled with paradox.

"They were filled with fear and great joy," Matthew tells us. Paradox. Can both be true at the same time? As we look around us this year in every corner of our globe, we find that to be true. We continue to listen to the Easter story "with fear and great joy." We Christians proclaim, once again, that we believe in the resurrection. What is resurrection?

In his book "Blessed Are You Who Believed," Carlos Carretto describes resurrection this way:

"When the world seems a defeat for God and you are sick with disorder, the violence, the terror, the war on the streets; when the earth seems to be in chaos, say to yourself, 'Jesus died and rose again on purpose to save, and his salvation is already with us.'

"When your father or your mother, your son or your daughter, your spouse or your friend are on their death bed, and you are looking at them in the pain of parting, say, 'We shall see each other again in the kingdom; courage.'

"Every departing missionary is an act of faith in the resurrection.

"Every newly opened hospital to treat those who have been sickened by the virus is an act of faith in the resurrection. Every mobile vaccination site where people roll up their shirt sleeves is an act of faith in the resurrection.

Every peace treaty is an act of faith in the resurrection. Every agreed commitment is an act of faith in the resurrection.

When you forgive your enemy, when you feed the hungry, when you defend the weak, when you give up your personal freedom so that another can live, you believe in the resurrection.

When you have the courage to marry, or you welcome the newborn child, when you build your home, you believe in the resurrection.

When you wake at peace in the morning. When you sing to the rising sun. When you go to work with joy, you believe in the resurrection." (Lent: The Sunday Readings, Megan McKenna p.212)

Christ is risen! Christ is risen indeed! Is it the end of the story or just the beginning? Wherever there is resurrection in the world, there is always plenty to say.

Fredrich Nietzsche, a 19th century philosopher, wrote about Christians and Christianity. He praised Christianity as a religion, but he never became a Christian. His answer, when questioned about this, was "For a group of people who claim to believe in the resurrection, none of them looks redeemed."

I must beg to differ with the old philosopher and dare to suggest that he must have been looking in all the wrong places.

Adds Roman Catholic scholar Megan McKenna, "The undeniable sign of resurrection is joy, looking redeemed, bringing a sense of hope to others that is tangible and irresistible. It is not shallow, but deep, abiding and enduring. Death cannot break its hold, and suffering and persecution often strengthen it. It brings light, and remembers to seek out the stars in the darkest part of the night. It knows fear, but is not paralyzed by it. It is hardnosed self-sacrifice knowledgeable of the razor edge of sin, and yet it knows how to sidestep, when to dance and when to run—and when to stand face to face and stare evil down and take its knife thrust. It shoulders the cross and denies itself, and turns toward the face of God in others." (op.cit. Lent: The Sunday Readings, p.213)

"And they were filled with fear, and great joy." There is PLENTY to say. Amen.

◆ ◆ ◆

Let us pray: O thou who didst rise again,
Thou Holy Spirit of Christ, arise and live
Within us now, that we may be thy body,
That we may be thy feet, to walk in the world's pain
Thy hands to heal, Thy heart to break,
If need must be, for the love of the world.
Thou risen Christ, make Christs of us all. Amen.
(Beuchner- "The Hungering Dark"-p.112)

Chapter 32

PASSING THE LOVE ALONG
(Mother's Day)

"Righteous Father, the world does not know you, but I know you; and these know that you have sent me. I made your name known to them, and I will make it known, so that the love with which you have loved me, may be in them, and I in them." (John 17:25-26)

Hen I hear these words of Jesus from St. John's Gospel, I can't help but think of parenting and all the hopes and dreams of both mothers and fathers for their children.

Some years ago, as a Christmas gift to Joan and our three daughters, with the help of a friend who is more computer savvy than I am, I put together some of the pieces of free verse poetry that I had written in a book I named, "Poems from a Father's Heart."

Each poem was about someone who had touched my life in a special way. Included were pictures from the past and some of the times we had shared together.

Joan is there, of course. And each of our girls. Even our puppy, Bridget Marie, made the book. Bridget was a part of our family for thirteen years. My mom was there. So was Joan's mom. And so was my dad. Joan's dad had died when she was very young, long before any of us got to know him.

I called the poem for my mother "Cookies, Milk, and Mom." It went like this:

"Not everybody's mother is the same. I was one of the blessed. I had a good one.

Oh, she wasn't perfect. Don't misunderstand. None of us are.
There were many times I went storming up the stairs and slammed the door.
Angered. Exasperated. Something that she'd said. To me, her perfect son.
I reacted much like our three girls, when they despaired of me, I'm sure.

Mom did some things. Said some things. That I would never understand.

But my mother gave to me the gift of affirmation.
I learned from her, how good it felt, when I had done things well.
Had gifts to share.
No one else had told me that until that time.

If it hadn't been for mom, I might not have known.
She believed in me.
That was how she shared her love for me.

So many times, she simply sat and listened,
To the rueful meanderings of her son.
After a long day at the Rubber Mills, she would tell me to sit down,
and
Share my day with her. No matter how mundane.

She made those moments feel important,
Over cookies, and some milk.

When I think of her, even now, it's 'cookies, milk and mom'
That come to mind.
Her love will never leave me. Though I scarcely knew it,
At the time."

When I look back at that little poem, I can only think, "Oh! It wasn't enough. I should have said more. So much more!"

What can you say about a person who has given you so much?

Jesus prayed, "So that the love with which you have given me may be in them."

I can only hope that the love she gave me I have passed along the way to others, so that they, in turn, might do the same to the people in their lives.

If you have ever been a mother, or a father, I am sure you have had regrets. Most of us do. Every now and then, I can't help but think of all the things I wished that I'd done differently as a parent. Oliver Wendell Holmes said something to the effect that "one of the great reliefs of life is to discover your own mediocrity." But mediocrity, he would add, does not mean insignificance. Significant contributions to the world do not wait to be done by perfect people. How is it that one poet put it? "How silent the woods would be if only the best birds sang."

In Marion Wright Edelman's best-selling book, "The Measure of our Success," she has a chapter entitled, "A Letter to My Sons." It includes the following remarkable paragraph:

"I seek your forgiveness for all the times when I should have listened; got angry when I should have been patient; acted when I should have waited; feared when I should have been delighted; criticized when I should have complimented; said no when I should have said yes, and yes, when I should have said no."

The fact is parenting doesn't come with an instruction book. I did not know a whole lot about parenting when I entered that role, nor did I even know how to ask for help. A lot of us tried too hard, demanded too much, and tried to mold our children into our image of what we wanted them to be, instead of standing beside them, loving unconditionally, as they began to discover what was always there, deep inside."

As a dad, I know that what Edelman writes is true for me. Is it too trite to say that "we can only do the best with what we have been given"? It sometimes takes us a long time to learn these things. We need to remind ourselves of that every day, and then move on from there.

Then we can say thank you. Thank you, Mom. Thank you, Dad. Thank you, God, for giving us a shot at this business of parenting about which we are still trying to learn. It is a rich and amazing journey.

♦ ♦ ♦

Let us pray: Let the love with which you have loved us in Jesus, O God, be with all of those with whom you have entrusted us. Center our lives in Christ, so that your love may always be passed along to others. In his name, we pray. Amen.

Chapter 33

IN THAT FINAL
WEEK IN MAY 2020

"He has told you, O mortal, what is good; and what does the Lord require of you, but to do justice, to love kindness, and to walk humbly with your God." (Micah 6:8)

It was a strange and unsettling week, that final week in the month of May 2020.

Oftentimes, it seems, this same week in our calendar year can bring with it the threat of violent storms – storms that loom in the western skies as the afternoon goes by and the evening enters in.

Often, too, those clouds bring with them sudden winds, like those on the Day of Pentecost in the lives of those who followed Jesus. Dangerous winds.

Not in 2020. Not right here in Minnesota, at least. That final week in May brought threats of another kind altogether.

These were silent storms that came from tiny droplets in the air that no one seemed to know were there.

COVID became a brand-new word for most of us. "Social distancing" was a phrase that we'd begun to say with ease.

We crossed the line that final week in May with 100,000 dead, here in the United States. 1,000 dead in the state that we call home. If only that had been the end of things.

But then on Tuesday, in that final week of May, all hell broke loose, literally. A young black man named George Floyd was killed by a Minneapolis policeman on the streets of the city. And the entire world watched on video. Our city erupted in that final week in May 2020. Hundreds of years of injustice and rage poured itself out in violence and destruction. Other cities followed, all around the world.

"I can't breathe," he said. "I can't breathe."

He said it until he couldn't say it anymore.

We ached for answers. We're aching still. Holding our breath. Wondering where and when and if it will happen all over again. Will we ever overcome some day?

We sang it once, that song, back in the sixties, but injustice had gone too deep, continued and spilled over, and now it had all come back again.

Our roofers had come that day, in that final week in May, as the world was boiling over. When they had finished, Joan and I tried to drag a bundle of roofing shingles into our garage to protect them from a coming storm. But our aging bodies weren't performing very well.

Have you ever tried to lift a bundle of shingles? I used to do it in my younger days. That day, I learned again that it's not for the faint of heart and body. At least not ours.

It was then that I heard a voice from the walking path that goes by our home.

"Do you need help with those?" the voice called out. A young man was walking by and saw us struggling. "Bless you my son," I said to myself. "That's very kind," I said out loud.

With ease, he grabbed those bundles of shingles, with a smile on his face, and hardly a grunt.

"Are you a weight lifter?" asked Joan, with gratitude in her voice.

"Nope. A gymnast," he said, "but they wouldn't let me join the school team," he openly declared, "because I'm gay."

"That's not fair!" I heard my wife respond.

"I hope that it will change some day," he said, with longing in his voice.

"So do I," said Joan. So did we both agree. After we thanked him for his kindness, he walked away.

After that we went inside, Joan and I, and watched the protests on the streets. But because of that young man, there was a flicker of hope in our hearts.

"I hope someday that will change," we thought that night. We'll hold our breath and hang on to that flicker of hope that we felt that night.

In that final week of May.

* * *

Let us pray. You have told us, O God, what is good. We asked, and you replied, when we wondered what the Lord required of us. Do justice. Love kindness. Walk humbly with you. Be thou our vision, O Lord. For in you we find our hope. We pray in your name. Amen.

Chapter 34

THAT'S HOW THE LIGHT GETS IN
(Independence Day)

"For I do not do the good I want, but the evil I do not want is what I do. Now, if I do what I do not want, it is no longer I that do it, but sin that dwells within me. For I delight in the law of God in my inmost self, but I see in my members another law at war with the law of my mind, making me captive to the law of sin that dwells in my members. Wretched man that I am! Who will rescue me from this body of death? Thanks be to God through Jesus Christ, our Lord! (Romans 7:19-25)

We are indeed living in troubled times! Unrest, discomfort, angry protests seem to be surrounding us. Can we ever find healing and peace in our world? I want these times to be the beginning a positive change, yet I find myself asking along with St. Paul, "who will rescue me (us) from this body of death?" The road ahead seems long and perilous.

"One of the most iconic symbols of the United States of America is Philadelphia's Liberty Bell. The bell is noted, of course, for its unsightly crack, which appeared just after its arrival in Philadelphia in 1752, as it was being rung for the very first time. The Whitechapel Foundry in London had delivered a flawed product!

What was to be done? Sending such a heavy object back across the Atlantic for repair was a daunting proposition. A couple of local foundry men, John Pass and John Stow, repaired the crack and inscribed their own names on its side.

All was well for several decades. The Liberty Bell called the members of the Continental Congress to their meetings, and it was very likely rung on July 8, 1776, to make the public reading of the Declaration of Independence. In 1835, as it was being rung to commemorate the death of Chief Justice John Marshall, the crack reappeared. This time it was not repaired.

In 1865, as President Abraham Lincoln's body lay in state in Independence Hall, the bell was placed near his head. The verse from Leviticus 25:10 inscribed on its side was visible to thousands of mourners who filed by: "Proclaim liberty throughout the world and to all inhabitants thereof."

Some may think it strange that such a cherished national symbol should be marred by an obvious flaw. Yet the flaw has now become a part of its character. It is emblematic of the country itself, which is not perfect. As the line from "O Beautiful for Spacious Skies" attests, as a nation we can only turn to God, asking that, by grace, the broken can be made whole.

'America, America, God mend thine every flaw,
Confirm thy soul, in self-control, Thy liberty in law.'"
(Homiletics – p.73, April 27, 2014)

I was heartened recently when I read the words of the great
Biblical scholar **Walter Breuggeman** who wrote:

"We are all of us, children of faith. We have been conceived
and birthed, generated and summoned, given life by faith and
none other. Faith keeps having its way among us. We must come
to terms with it. We spend our lives struggling with faith, sometimes struggling for faith, sometimes struggling against faith.
Faith always has its say among us. It will not go away. Its voice
is a haunting one. And in it we hear the very voice of God; ma-
jestic sovereignty. Awesome holiness, passionate grace, weakness made strong. We have haunted lives filled with yearnings
for what is not in hand, promises not yet filled, commands not
yet obeyed, desires not yet granted, neighbors not yet loved, and
because faith will not go away or be silent, we are destined to be
endlessly haunted. Uneasy, on the way." (The Clergy Journal,
May/June 2001)

That crack in our Liberty Bell is a reminder of the crack that
runs through all of humanity. As St. Paul reminds us, "We can
will what is right, but we cannot do it. For I do not do the good
that I want, but the evil I do not want is what I do." We hardly
need to point the finger at anyone else, unless we begin by pointing it at ourselves. We are not perfect, and there is no perfect nation. There is a crack in everything.

So, let us look boldly into the heart of the crack. And then, in faith, let us look to the one who came to rescue us from this body of death. The one who came to make all things new.

Not long ago, dear friends of ours brought to our attention the haunting song by Leonard Cohen:

The birds they sang at the break of day,
"Start again," I heard them say.
"Don't dwell on what has passed away,
Or what is yet to be."

"Ring the bells, that still can ring.
Forget your perfect offering.
There is a crack, a crack, in everything,
That's how the light gets in.

"Ah, the holy wars they will be fought again,
The holy dove she will be caught again,
Bought and sold and bought again,
The dove is never free."

"So, ring the bells that still can ring,
Forget your perfect offering.
There is a crack, a crack, in everything,
That's how the light gets in."

* * *

Let us pray: As we wonder, Lord, who will rescue us from this body of death, we look to you. Continue to haunt us in faith, dear Christ, as we struggle in these troubled times. May we look deeply into the crack, and behold "the light of the world." We pray in your name. Amen.

Chapter 35

FOR WE DO NOT KNOW

"Likewise, the Spirit helps us in our weakness; for we do not know how to pray as we ought, but that very Spirit intercedes with sighs too deep for words. And God, who searches the heart, knows what is the mind of the Spirit, because the Spirit intercedes for the saints according to the will of God." (Romans 8:26-27)

There is a very small portion of that wonderful chapter of St. Paul's letter to the Romans that got stuck in my mind as I read it.

It was the words, "for we do not know." We do not even know "how to pray as we ought," the great apostle writes.

Perhaps those words stuck with me more than any of the others because time and time again it seems there is just so much "we do not know."

That has been especially true as some of the greatest minds in our scientific world struggled to find some answers for what came to be called COVID-19, the pandemic of 2020.

Some said it would eventually go away. Others said it was no worse than a really bad cold or the flu. Others predicted horrific and startling implications. We now know that way too many people already have lost their lives because of it here in the United States, and more worldwide. These little germs have wreaked their havoc all around the world. Some would say the psychological and economic damage was just as devastating as the physical damage, if not more so.

As I write this, we have at least three very promising vaccines that seem to have proven effective in treating COVID-19. There is a promise of even more.

Now another question raises its ugly head. How in the world can we convince people to take it? How will we distribute it to the millions of people in our world whose lives it continues to threaten, and who should be given priority? How can we do this fairly and equitably within and beyond our own borders? What can I do to protect myself and others?

"For we do not know." Those words have become our collected mantra as we try to come to grips with all of these uncertainties.

In the Old Testament, when the Lord asks the new King Solomon what it is he would ask for as he begins his reign after his father David's death, he replies, "Give your servant an understanding mind to govern your people, able to discern between good and evil." (I Kings 3: 9) But even with the explosion of scientific knowledge that has occurred ever since those Old Testament times, we are still making that request of God to this day.

"What is good? And what is evil?" Those questions never seem to go away. Whether it's the pandemic of 2020, or how we deal with racial injustices, or how we are going to feed our famished world, or how we can save ourselves from completely destroying ourselves and everything in it, or how we can best protect and love our own families, we just "do not always know."

So, let's begin right there, by simply saying those words, "We do not know" and then go on to pray, "How can we know the way?" Yet, at the same time recognizing the fact that as St. Paul reminds us, "We do even know how to pray as we ought."

As Professor James Limburg reflected on the 23rd Psalm in his book "Psalms for the Sojourner," he remembered a time when his young son had received his first 10-speed bicycle:

"It was a Sunday afternoon in the springtime, and we took a ride on the bike path around our town. Just off the path was a drainage tunnel which ran under the interstate highway. We decided to explore it. We parked our bikes and began to walk through the tunnel.

"It was made of concrete, wide enough for us to walk side by side, but not high enough for me to stand up straight. We walked for a distance and then the tunnel took a sharp turn, and suddenly it became dark. A hand reached out and took mine. Neither of us said anything about it, but we continued, hand in hand, until we came to another turn and we could see the light. Then the hand let go.

"The 23rd Psalm is a Psalm for those times when life takes a sharp turn and leads through the darkness," writes the wise professor. "There is no hint that we can avoid the dark valley by taking a detour around

it. The path will have to be traveled. But there is a promise that we will never have to go through the darkness alone. There is a hand that we can reach out to hold as we grow through these times. 'For thou art with me. Thy rod and thy staff they comfort me.'" (Psalm 23:4)

There is so much that we do not know. Yet even in these times, the great apostle reminds us what we *do* know. What we do know is that God is in the midst of our "not knowing." God is there, in the midst of all our uncertainties and fears, and the only certainty we need flows from God's own divine initiative to claim us as his own through our Lord Jesus Christ.

So, we tilt our heads, we cup our ears, then listen to the conclusion of this same great chapter of Romans.

"Who will separate us from the Love of Christ? Will hardship, or distress, or persecution, or famine, or nakedness, or peril or sword? No! In all these things we are more than conquerors through him who loved us. For I am convinced that neither death, nor life, nor angels, nor rulers, nor things present, nor things to come, nor powers, nor height, nor depth, nor anything else in all creation shall be able to separate us from the love of God in Christ Jesus our Lord." (Romans 8: 35-36, 37-39)

That much we *do* know. We *do* believe. Thanks be to God!

♦ ♦ ♦

Let us pray: Even when the world around us grows dark, when we are unable to see, take our hand, precious Lord. Show us the way that leads to the light of your son. We pray in his name. Amen.

Chapter 36

FOR THE GREATER GOOD

*"This is my commandment, that you love one another as
I have loved you. No one has greater love than this, to
lay down his life for one's friends." (John 15: 12-13)*

In the cover story of the Washington Post National Weekly,
there appeared an article recently that was called, quite
simply, "For the Greater Good."

My definition of a hero seems to be constantly changing
these days. While it seems that the pandemic of 2020 has brought
out the worst in us, it has also brought out the best.

The article appeared on February 7, 2021. There was a picture
included there of a giant, black-haired, black-bearded handsome
man, who appeared to be deep in thought, pondering deeply, as
if struggling with significant life choices and considering all the
alternatives.

His name is **Laurent Duvernay-Tardif.** He is 6'6" tall. He
weighs 321 pounds. Months earlier, he had blocked for Patrick
Mahomes in Super Bowl LIV. He had celebrated after the game

in front of 62,000 fans after the Chief's victory. Now, he was surrounded by nervous and exhausted colleagues at an 8:30 a.m. staff meeting and listened to a somber update.

The coronavirus outbreak at the hospital had worsened. No staff members could take vacation for seven months. Many of them would be forced to work overtime. Duverny-Tardif saw some of his colleagues cry. Ten minutes later, they were back at the bedsides of patients, most of whom were sick and dying, offering comfort as best they could with smiles on their faces.

"The definition of what it means to be a hero changed because of those people," the big man said. "If I am to take risks, I will do it caring for patients," he said.

In July, shortly before training camps opened, Duverny-Tardif opted out of the NFL season so he could work at the COVID-19-stricken long-term care facility near his native Montreal, putting to use the medical degree he earned from McGill University. He traded his helmet for a mask and face shield.

It was an agonizing decision. He wondered what his future in the NFL would be if he sat out. He feared letting down his teammates. Cases had started to subside by late summer; what if he opted out for no reason? He ultimately chose not to play for the entire season, even as he watched his teammates come closer and closer to playing in another Super Bowl. He had no idea if there would be a place for him on the team next year, even if the virus subsided.

He convinced himself he made the right choice. The virus again exploded in the United States, and it invaded several locker rooms, including that of the Chiefs. His football career will last a few more years, at most, and the rest of his life he will be with

doctors and medical workers. They will know the most conse-
quential choice of his professional career erred on the side of
medicine. "But who knows how I'm going to feel in 10 years?"
he said.

He had traded working on one "front line" for another. He
has become a hero for me.

But Laurent Duvernay-Tardif is not alone. Not by any means.
He is big and strong and very bright. He is a man with many
talents. But he is just one of many who have given of themselves
to risk their lives day by day as this global pandemic continues
to stalk the world.

In the corridors of hospitals, nursing homes and primary care
facilities everywhere, emergency responders stand ready to put
their lives on the line when the alarm is sounded. Teachers, who
are trying their best to educate our children safely under the most
trying of circumstances, not knowing if and when they do they,
too, might become infected. They are my heroes.

Some of the brightest and best in science have worked day
and night trying to find the right vaccine that will save the lives
of thousands. And now they have. Now others are seeking to find
ways to make sure those vaccines get into our bodies, in what
must seem like an insurmountable task. Heroes. Too many to
mention.

Is it a little thing to wear a mask to protect yourself and others? Those who do are my heroes, too. It has become a huge financial crisis for so many in business trying to earn a living even
as their businesses are shuttered, heroes all.

They are giving their lives for the greater good. Bless them.

We pray for them today, that they might be given courage for the days ahead.

We want them to know how thankful we are for everything they do for all of us.

♦   ♦   ♦

Let us pray: For personal sacrifices that so many have made and continue to make each day, dear Lord, as we face these challenges around us. Give these heroes strength. Give them courage, as they continue to strive for the greater good that we may have hope. In Jesus' name. Amen.

Chapter 37

WHEN MONDAY ROLLS AROUND

*"For by the grace given to me, I say to everyone among
you not to think of yourself more highly than you ought
to think, but to think with sober judgment, each according to the measure that God has assigned."*
(Romans 12:3)

Today, we are urged by the apostle Paul not to "think of
ourselves more highly than we ought to think."

I think the place to begin when we consider these
words is with ourselves. Pretty easy to see how those words ap-
ply to others, don't you think?

All I have to do when I start to think of myself as "pretty hot
stuff" is to pick up a set of golf clubs. Very humbling. Very humbling, indeed! Thinking of ourselves more highly than we ought
to think is usually a pretty good place to begin to get ourselves
in a lot of trouble.

One very honest politician in a recently aired interview with ABC News, blamed his own fall from grace on what he called, "a self-focus, an egotism, a narcissism, that led him to believe that he could do whatever he wanted, whenever he wanted." It's happening today. It's been happening for a long, long time.

One of the most respected theologians of the twentieth century, Reinhold Niebuhr, has suggested that in our walk through life as human beings we are constantly being tempted to become either more or less than the person God intended us to be when we were created to live on this earth. How easy it seems to be when you hear thousands of people cheering the moment you step on the stage to believe you must be a very incredible person. At the same time, when things begin to go badly, how easy it is to get down on yourself and to begin to believe that you really have no reason to be on this earth in the first place. Niebuhr would call this "the human predicament." It is only through faith, the great theologian would say, that it's possible for us to live within that tension of wanting to be, and believing yourself to be, either more or less than what God intended you to be.

We are called to live a life of "integrity," a word that's bantered about all over the place these days. But just what does it look like?

Writes Jay Marshall, "A call for integrity is a call for consistency between our beliefs and our actions, between our words and our deeds. Integrity gives evidence – evidence that our lives demonstrate the convictions, the commitments, and loyalties we claim to embrace. From a faith perspective, integrity shows congruence between the lives we live and the values and expectations we adopt in our spiritual journey, whether we identify with a particular tradition or not." (Alive Now, September/October 2008)

In a little piece in that same issue of "Alive Now," that she calls "When Monday Rolls Around," Andrea Woods tells us about Mr. Pritchett.

*Mr. Pritchett didn't talk much—he mostly listened. And when that man listened, he **really** listened, all the way into the middle of the story, and back out again. His words were few, and he had a tendency to say pretty much the same thing, over and over again. But when he did decide to talk, everybody leaned forward a little bit and sat up a little straighter, straining to hear every word.*

What Mr. Pritchett said more often than anything else was this: "I don't care where you go to church on Sunday morning, or how you sing your songs. It don't matter to me how you take up the offering or whether you get baptized by 'dippin' or 'sprinklin.' What I do care about is what you do with Sunday when Monday rolls around.

The young folks didn't have to wonder what became of Mr. Pritchett's own Sunday during the week. They saw it each and every day of his life.

If a widow in the community had a broken window, Mr. Pritchett would somehow learn about it and show up with his tool box in his hand. When anybody got sick, from close friends to mere acquaintances, he would volunteer to drive them to the doctor, sit with the family in the waiting room, or bring from his garden whatever was ripening on the vine at home.

There wasn't an ounce of guile or sarcasm in Mr. Pritchett. His sense of humor ran to chuckles about the antics of squirrels and blue jays, or gentle self-deprecation about his own supposed errors. And you couldn't make him mad. It seems as if Mr. Pritchett was just congenitally incapable of flying into a temper, or even yelling out a cuss word, the way so many adults seemed to when things went a little bit wrong.

Everyone who worked with Mr. Pritchett used to tell him their troubles and ask his advice about decisions they were considering. Even when he just listened without advising, they felt better having talked with him. And more often than not, they emerged with a little cash in their pockets to help them through whatever crisis was current at the moment.

What the young folks saw in Mr. Pritchett was a life that was all of one piece, whole and entire, from the head to the hands, from the heart to the mouth. The Monday man at work was exactly the same as the Sunday man at worship. Mr. Pritchett, seventh grade graduate, one of the best teachers young folks ever had." (op.cit., p. 16-18)

"I say to everyone among you, not to think of yourself more highly than you ought to think, but to think with sober judgment, each according to the measure that God has assigned." (Romans 12:3)

I wonder – could we nominate Mr. Pritchett for something? We need more of him to lead our world.

◆　◆　◆

Let us pray: It's not a perfect world, dear God. Nor are we perfect people. Each of us struggles with our choices to be more or less than we were meant to be. Be with us when our Monday's roll around, so that our Sunday world will be right there with us. In Jesus' name. Amen.

Chapter 38

A BRIEF BUT
SPECTACULAR MOMENT

"Let love be genuine, hate what is evil, hold fast to what is good. Love one another with mutual affection; outdo one another in showing honor." (Romans 12:9-10)

It's not a very long verse, but there are probably a hundred sermons that could come out of these few words from the Apostle Paul.

It sounds trite to say, but we are living in challenging times. I am sure you could say that about most of the days of our lives, but we all know about the added stress this worldwide pandemic has put on all of us. Especially the elderly and those who love them.

An article first appeared in the Op/Ed pages of the Minneapolis Star/Tribune on August 4, 2020. The author, Scott Bengston, titled it, "A brief magic moment shared amid chaos."

The author tells about his recent visit to a senior care facility where both of his parents reside in a memory care unit. His mom and dad had been separated for the last four months due to various problems associated with the dementia that has ravaged their lives. Those same issues had been haunting them for more than four years. They are both in their 90s, and they've been married for 70 years. The separation has been heartbreaking to both of them and all their family members. "Add that," the author writes, "to the COVID mess, and the word 'overwhelming' applies."

Scott Bengston realized the need for his parents to see each other face to face while they still were able. Time was growing short. His request was granted, thanks to the staff at their long-term care facility.

Here is how he describes it: "It was a gorgeous summer morning. The temperatures were in the high 70s, and a light breeze was blowing. It took place in a small out-door tent-like structure with appropriate anti-COVID measures."

He wondered whether his 92-year-old mother would show up and have a bad day with memory loss, loss of muscle control and loss of thought process. He was filled with angst. He wondered if his dad would show up wracked with confusion and a belligerent demeanor.

His article described how the caregiver brought his mother out first, very slowly, carefully guiding her elaborate wheelchair to the tent. Whenever the wheelchair would hit a small bump, his mom would whimper with pain. She now weighed about 70 pounds. She could speak only two or three words at a time. He wasn't sure if she recognized him anymore. She appeared to be conscious of things around her.

He loudly said, "Hi Mom, how's it going?" She did not reply. He sat alone with her in the COVID tent.

About five minutes later, the caregiver came back to the tent with his 91-year-old father. He walked very slowly, with difficulty. He had refused to use a walker despite pleas from the caregivers. He had suffered a stroke two years before that had left the right side of his body partly paralyzed. He could no longer use his right hand, so he had to learn to eat with his left hand. "Food," Scott said, "is important to Dad."

He's had good days and bad days. The author had no idea what this day would bring.

Laura, the caregiver, carefully walked up with his dad in the COVID tent where an empty chair was placed next to his mom in her wheelchair. His mom was awake, but she did not see his dad, since she can't see much.

"Dad instantly recognized his wife of 70 years, and a look of amazement filled his face. He said nothing at first, just slowly walked over to his mom. He very gently placed his hands on her hands and said, 'Hi Patti, how are you doing?' He then gently kissed her.

Mom recognized Dad's voice and lifted her head up to try to see him through her blind eyes. Her face was aglow. She replied, 'Good!'

For about thirty seconds, they simply stared at each other with bright smiles and a love developed over the 70 years they had been together. The sunlight filtered through the tree branches above as the light breeze washed over us."

For about 30 seconds, the author said, there was no dementia, no COVID-19, no hate, no racism, no partisan politics. For about 30 seconds, the world was perfect.

Very little was spoken over the next half hour. His parents simply stared at each other and held hands.

Laura eventually came back and gently took his father back to his apartment. Then she came back to fetch his mother, who looked very happy and tired.

"Those thirty seconds," the author said, "meant the world to me." (Minneapolis Star/Tribune op ed., August 4, 2020)

"Let love be genuine. Hate what is evil. Hold fast to what is good. Love one another with mutual affection, out-do one another in showing honor." (Romans 12:9-10)

It was British author J.R.R. Tolkien who once said, "It is the small everyday deeds of folk that keep the darkness away. Small acts of kindness and love."

◆ ◆ ◆

Let us pray: Hold before us always, dear God, the grace notes of your kingdom. Genuine love. A determination to do battle with the evils that surround us, holding fast to the hope that is ours. In Jesus' name. Amen.

Chapter 39

OCTOBER SURPRISE

"You who live in the shelter of the Most High, who abide in the shadow of the Almighty, will say to the Lord, 'My refuge and my fortress; my God in whom I put my trust.'" (Psalm 91: 1-2)

I'm old enough to remember the Halloween blizzard of '91.

Now here we are again!

October of 2020.

As if a global pandemic weren't enough to get our attention! Apocalyptic days and times surely are upon us.

Sort of makes us wonder, what next?

The Psalmist wonders, "How long, O Lord, must we seek the shelter of your arms?'

"The snow is gorgeous!" my optimistic bride of many years can say.

(I need to keep her around a while. She often sees what I cannot!)

Hurricanes. Earthquakes. Tsunamis. Fires. And Floods. A national election unlike any other!!

But don't you think we've had enough for a while, Lord?

"Shelter us in your arms once more.

Now and always, and into forever.

But don't forget to wear your face mask!"

(Terry R. Morehouse, Oct. 19, 2020)

Chapter 40

THE STEADFAST LOVE

"I will sing of your steadfast love, O Lord, forever; with my mouth I will proclaim your faithfulness to all generations. I declare that your steadfast love is established forever; your faithfulness is as firm as the heavens." *(Psalm 89: 1-2)*

During the quarantine days surrounding the pandemic of 2020, Joan and I spent a lot of time together. So much happened during those days, and not very much of it was happy. Many of us were on the edge of sadness. Each day seemed to bring more of the same.

One night we watched the movie version of "Fiddler on the Roof."

It might have been the umpteenth time we've seen it. Whether at the Ordway in St. Paul, at a high school production in our home town, or at the Chanhassen Dinner Theater, it was always a treat.

Each time we have seen it, we have been enchanted by Tevye and Golda, the Papa and the Mama and their five daughters, who all lived in the tiny village of Anatevka in the days just before the Russian revolution.

Songs like "Tradition, Tradition!," "If I Were a Rich Man," "Matchmaker, Matchmaker," and "Do You Love Me?" always seemed to bring a smile and make us want to sing along.

On this night, however, what struck us was how sad the story is. I'm sure the pandemic that surrounded our world right then had something to do with that. The song that Tevye sings as he watches three of his daughters fall in love with three young men – young men who seem to be so far from what he and his wife had hoped and dreamed for their daughters – probably captures the sadness more than any other. Remember?

Sunrise, sunset,
Swiftly flow the days.
Seedlings turn overnight to sunflowers,
Blossoming, even as we gaze.

Sunrise sunset,
Swiftly fly the years.
One season following another,
Laden with happiness and tears.

Is this the little girl I carried?
Is this the little boy at play?
I don't remember growing older,
When did they?

What words of wisdom can I give them?
How can I help to ease their way?
Now they must learn from one another,
Day by day.

Sunrise, sunset,
Swiftly fly the years.
One season following another,
Laden with happiness,
And tears.

Part of the reason I was so struck with the sadness of the story more than at any other time was because all the other times had been a live production, not a movie. As you know, at the end of a live production, the entire cast comes out on stage to take their bows, with great smiles, with thunderous applause, and everyone seems so happy.

But at the end of the movie version, we watched this beloved family and their friends and neighbors trudge out of their tiny village, victims of the Russian revolution, with all of their meager possessions in tow, knowing that many of them would never see each other again. They were still singing, "Sunrise, Sunset," but there was no thunderous applause. We only saw the credits on the screen with the music playing softly in the background. Inhabitants of the entire village left their homes and everything they had built their lives on. As the Biblical writer puts it, they went out "not knowing." (Hebrews 11)

Yet, despite all their changes and all their broken dreams, they knew and still believed in the ancient promises.

How did our Psalm for today put it?

I will sing of your steadfast love, O Lord, forever;
With my youth I will proclaim your faithfulness
To all generations.
I declare that your steadfast love is established,
Forever.

Tevye and Golda hung on to the faith that had led them in the past and would lead them now, even as they "stepped out, not knowing."

Sunrise, sunset,
Swiftly fly the years.
One season following another,
Laden with happiness and tears.

And in the midst of all of our tumultuous days, especially as we seek to rediscover what normalcy means, let us remember those ancient promises as well.

"Let them come," those days of change, the poet says, "as they will, and don't be afraid. God does not leave us comfortless, so let evening come." (Jane Kenyon, "Beloved on Earth")

♦   ♦   ♦

Let us pray: Our hearts are restless, Lord, until they find their rest in you. Grant that we might believe in you, call upon you, know you and serve you through all our days. In the name of our Savior, Jesus Christ, we pray. Amen.

Chapter 41
WHILE THERE IS TIME

"Owe no one anything, except to love one another, for the one who loves another has fulfilled the law. Besides this, you know what time it is, how it is now time for you to wake from your sleep. For salvation is nearer to us now than when we became believers; the night is far gone, the day is near." (Romans 13: 8,11-12)

I thought for a long, long time about what I might share with those who had so faithfully listened as I brought my years on Faith Alive to a close. It's never easy to say good-bye.

I started doing this program for our church in January of 1994. Yet, in some ways, it seems like yesterday. Joan and I celebrated 56 years of marriage in August of 2020, and even those years seem to have whisked right by.

St. Paul writes: "Besides this, you know what time it is."

I'll try not to get too blubbery, but if you see some damp spots on this page, you'll know I didn't quite make it.

"The night is far gone," the apostle continues in our text today, "The day is near." (13:12)

Some time ago, I discovered an author by the name of William Joyner. His book was entitled, "Wheels in the Air," and it was published in 1968. It's a book of free verse poetry that I keep coming back to over and over again. I share with you now one of his poems that I continue to ponder after all this time. He calls it, "While There is Time."

Each morning
The sun greets the earth,
Kissing its open face
With life.

And as it clings to the warmth,
Each spot of soil
Is seduced to believe
That its bright visitor
Is there to stay.

But in vain,
For soon
As always,
The voice of evening
Whispers from some darkening place.
"Your time is up."

"Your time is up!"
Who knows the meaning

Of those staggering words?
Perhaps a chosen people of antiquity,
  Who, when the time was ripe
  Heard them fall from Nazarene lips.

Or maybe, we ourselves,
  When in some yesterday.
  We saw a valued person,
  Perhaps a maturing child,
  Slipping beyond us.

Then we discovered the sound,
  Of the last judgement:
  Your time is up!

Today, just for an instant,
  There is time
  To cast light and warmth
  Into the dark corners.
  To salt the earth.

But who knows
  For how long?

Who ever knows,
  How much time remains
  Before the Lord of time will come?
  Like some teacher collecting papers
  And say:

"*Friend,*

Your time is up." (Joyner-Pilgrim's Press, "Wheels in the Air")

Now, I know that all sounds rather ominous. It's not intended that way. Just a reminder that time has a way of getting away from us. And to be reminded that "just for an instant, there *is* time, to cast light and warmth. Into the dark corners.

To salt the earth."

"The night is far gone, the day is at hand," writes the apostle.

As I struggle to say good-bye, to say thank you to all of you, and to be of good courage, and as we hear the desperate cries for justice and peace that surround us, as we feel the tensions of a great political divide in our nation, we are left with a great challenge.

To love one another. To live honorably and honestly. And while there is time, even for just an instant, "to cast light and warmth into the dark corners of the earth." As disciples of the one who is called "the Christ," that is our most important task.

God speed, fellow travelers. And "Shalom!"

♦ ♦ ♦

Let us pray: You have shown us, O Lord, a better way. Give us the courage and the strength to be your disciples in this world. In Jesus' name. Amen.

SECTION 4
LEAVES FROM A
PASTOR'S NOTE BOOK

Chapter 42

TO LOVE TOO MUCH

Is it wrong to love too much?
"Love God, with all your heart,
   Your soul, your mind,
   Your strength,
And your neighbor as yourself,"
The Bible says!

But when you love too much,
You lie awake at night, and worry.
   Or awaken with a start.
   You check their beds,
   To see if they are there and breathing.
Then you wait, with stomach growing tighter—
Every second. Nightmares in your mind, Irrational.
   If you love too much.

Is it wrong to love too much?

It can be, if you don't allow the ones you love,
    To grow, and to become.
It hurts so much to love too much.

But would I have it any other way?

Ah...if I could find the line that's drawn between
    The loving and the over love,
    That's where I would rest.
I'd write it down, hold it gently on my chest.

But since I can't, I'll simply have to bear the pain,
Then hope one day they'll understand.

Chapter 43

HUGS FOR SALE

I saw a sign the other day.

In town.

A gigantic sign, with the heightened words,

'HUG SALE"!

An arrow, pointing down the block.

Obviously the "E" was missing from

the first word on the sign.

It made me think, "I hope it never comes to that!"

That is,

"I hope we never have to buy them!"

We need those hugs so desperately!

To melt the hatred in our hardened hearts.

To fill our lives with meaning,

Warmth.

The tangible and outward sign that

There are those who care.

It's been a long and trying test of kindness and civility.

Once this year and all its trials are over,
Be sure, my friends, when you can, to hug someone today.
Free of charge.

Your spouse, your kids, your mom and dad, friends,
And, God forbid, someone you've had words with!
For the sale is ending soon!

Oh...and by the way, don't forget your pastor!

Chapter 44

ON A SUNDAY AFTERNOON

"There will be a time when you will begin to doubt everything I say."

That's how I began to write my weekly column to the congregation.

Try this one for instance.
While taking a walk on a Sunday afternoon,
Your pastor-- was attacked—by wild turkeys!

See…now there.
You're convinced I've flipped my lid.
"We've got to get that boy some help." you thought,
"as you began to read this column."

But wait a minute. I'm serious.
A lot of you didn't believe me when I told you
I spent one Christmas Eve in Boondocks, Iowa.

That, too, was true…but there are doubters still!

Strolling along, all by myself, minding my own business,
On a Sunday afternoon.
Turning off the gravel road, into a grove of pine trees,
enjoying the protection from the wind,
—when there they were!
Two tom turkeys coming after me!

At first, I thought, "well that's a fun discovery!"
Right here, in a Minnesota woods, very close to home. Wild
turkeys!
Then I discovered what they had in mind!
They didn't like me! It wasn't personal, was it?
(I'm a slow learner. Their hens were right close by.)

I must have been a funny sight, on that Sunday afternoon.
Talking to, shouting at, two tom turkeys, telling them to heel!
Then running home. My heart was pounding!

I don't know, I thought to myself.
There are just too many things,
They fail to teach in seminary.
They told me "not to let the turkeys get you down."
I just never expected to have to take it literally.

Chapter 45

PULL TABS FOR SALE

So read the sign just outside the Embassy,
>Bar and Grill.
>Now boarded up, and closed,
>Not far from where we have our cabin.

There is an essential kind of sadness in that sign.

Drawing images, of folks, seated — at a smoke-filled bar,
On a Sunday afternoon.
Tearing open tiny bits of paper.
Hoping, they'll be declared a winner.

If only they could know, that they've been so declared,
>Years ago.
>That God had chosen them.

If only they could see,

Or someone soon would tell them,
Before their lives have faded.

Lost… beneath the smoky haze
    of a Sunday afternoon.

Chapter 46

A TRAVELER IN THE NIGHT

He wandered in…from off the streets.

It was a place where the late-night lights still were shining.

"I have no place to stay," he said.

A friend had kicked him out.

So now in the deep freeze cold of winter,

There was no place for him to go.

And where is home?

What does it mean to a vagrant lad of 20?

His mother lives in Utah,

His friends here have abandoned him.

No suitcase or possessions.

No plans and no directions,

For tomorrow or beyond.

Where is home for this traveler in the night?

Home could be an entry way in the local city hall.

Any place that's warm.

Where hope could come
With morning light.

And where do I fit in?
Is there a place for me within his life tonight?
It's been a fourteen-hour day!
But I have a place to stay,
A place where people care, where I am loved.
A place that's warm.
Should I have to deal with this?

You keep asking me these terrible questions Lord!

When was it that we saw you a stranger, and welcomed you?
Or naked and clothed you? Or sick or in prison, and visited you?
They will haunt me
When the late-night lights can still be seen,
In the deep freeze cold of winter,
And whenever strangers wander, hungry and alone. (Matthew 25 - Terry R. Morehouse 1989)

Chapter 47

THE VOICELESS VOICE

"The heavens are telling the glory of God,"
  They are the words of Psalm 19.
"The firmament declares his handiwork!"

"There is no speech, nor are there words,"
this Psalm proclaims.
Yet still their voice is heard,
Going out to the ends of the earth.

It is the voiceless voice of heaven,
  That even the deaf can hear.
  Listen. (Terry R. Morehouse, October 1996)

Chapter 48

THE EAGLE

"You have seen what I did—how I bore you up, on eagles wings, and brought you to myself." (Exodus 19:4)

Statuesque—the eagle waits.
High—
Above the trees and waters,
Of his wilderness existence.

A sudden thrust! The tree tops tremble,
Released!
To soar, to stretch,
To seek the vault of heaven.

I have always dreamed of flying,
Only then to be awakened.
Disappointed, feet still planted,
Firmly on the ground.

"Lord…what must it be like?
To seek the drafts, to feel the shifts,
  To climb above the clouds,
  To know such freedom as this awesome bird of prey?

Life gets way too heavy, Lord!
Take our burdens, lift them up.
  On eagle's wings,
  Free us from our weariness,

And teach us,
  How to fly!" Amen. (Terry R. Morehouse, 1989)

Chapter 49

LITTLE GIRLS AND COOKIES

I guess that every man must think that his wife
    Is the very best cook
    That God has taken from his rib.
Especially when he steps on the scale
And hates himself for what he's done.

I do know that long ago,
There were some little girls
    Who lived close by,
    Who would concur with me,
    Whole heartedly.

"There are no better cookies made
By any mom around," they'd say.
    "Mrs. Morehouse, I just love your cookies!"
    That was Barbie, and she's grown now.

Days were simple then, or so it seems right now.
Days when little girls and cookies roamed the land.
They would come and go from our house,
Like the dampness of the morning dew,
On early morning dandelions.

So much has changed!
Little girls having babies.
Future cookie eaters of the world.

We sometimes grieve to watch them grow,
And make their choices.
We hope that they will always find
The love—that fills their emptiness.
Just like it seemed
That cookies
Used to do.

We pray that we could give them
All they need, as easily as the cookies
And the love
Of yesterday. (Dedicated to our neighbors and friends Barbie
and Becky Schneewind)

Chapter 50

THE REAL ME?

"I wanted to be what I thought,
You'd expected me to be.
And being who I am now, and always, is--
The greatest risk in the world." (Anonymous)

I'm not too sure who said it, but I've sometimes wondered,
    About the me I see myself being,
    And the me I actually am inside.
Especially on a Sunday morning.

How do other people see me then, this pastor of theirs?
Greeting people (warmly I think)
With great big smiles and "Good mornings!" "How are you
today?"
So many "So nice to see you!"s I want to gag sometimes.

If I weren't the pastor of this congregation
Would I be so friendly and exuberant?
Is the "role" I play, the me I feel?
Or is it just another game?
So, I get paid.
Affirmed
For being such a nice and caring pastor.

Sometimes I feel like the world's biggest phony!
Putting on a pious face
To cover up the anger and depression—Born of disappointments,
And the pain within.

Yet who I *really* am is hardly ever clear.
There are so *many* different m*e*s in there!
There IS a me who cares, who loves,
even though I may not always feel so loving.

God help me to be honest with myself,
Risky though it be.

Chapter 51

MODERN CABINS

"Modern Cabins" read the sign.
We almost missed it as we drove along.
These--the shores of pristine beauty,
Winding their ways along the shoals
Of Lake Superior.

It was the kind of place that we'd been looking for.
Primitive and simple.
A winding driveway off the highway led us to a place,
Where shivering sprays of ice blue water
Gaily splashed and played.
The pounding surf—ocean like,
Sounding forth, a soothing, steady rhythm.

Just four cabins made with rough cut logs,
Nestled in a cove. Exactly what we had in mind!
But we were puzzled.
Other places on our way had "no vacancy" signs out front.

Yet here it was, a prettier place we could not imagine.
But it was empty. Not a soul. Almost spooky!
Shades of "Psycho."
Austere and lonely.

Only in reflection did we think we found the reason.
No TV. No video games. No pool. No whirlpool or sauna.
No restaurant or bar—no matching drapes, or linen cloths,
No crystal cups or saucers.
These, it seems, are those which draw us in.

Here?
There was just the shore, the crashing of the waves,
The cool fresh air, the restless sound of winds, all night long,
Blowing through the pines.

Nothing more. Nothing less.
We stayed. God's peace was here.
The amenities were priceless.
(*Terry R. Morehouse, August 1989*)

Chapter 52

HOME

Tears in my eyes,
Music softly playing,
While just outside the cabin window,
Tufts of snow came falling down.

"Homecoming"—and yes,
Of all the places we've called home,
This one comes the closest to
Our dreams.

Modest, not precocious.
A place to snuggle in,
    To be alone
    Or be together,
Blanketed by memories,
Blessed with hopeful dreams.

"Home,"
or so they say,
Is "where the heart is."

If you're at the center of the place,
Where you can simply be, undeniably,
The one whom you were meant to be…
Then I believe---
That's where "home" is.

I must be there.

Chapter 53
CHARACTERS

Saturday…and looking out my office window,
   In a wistful sort of way,
An old green Ford reached out
   To catch my eye.
   It settled there to stay.

"At least a fifty-three" I thought,
   "At most a fifty-five."
The rusty sides betrayed at least a dozen winters
   That old, old car,
   Had struggled to survive.
Was there really someone there behind the wheel?
  Her head was bent. Her hair was white as snow.
"My word!" my mind exclaimed at first.
   "They shouldn't let her drive!
   She's dangerous, and everyone must know!"

I waited and I watched---for what seemed to be forever.
  Slowly then, the old Ford's door began to open.
One leg. Then another. I could feel the pain.
  Her hinges creaked, just like her car.
Reaching first to find her purse, then her cane,
A movie in slow motion.

Musing long and drinking deep in silent meditation
  I marveled at the wonder of it all.
An old, old Ford. Her driver?
A woman who was older than us all!
"This could only happen here," I reasoned,
  In Princeton, Minnesota.
Or another little town, in anywhere USA.

People simply seemed to know, to just be careful.
It's Saturday.
And grandma's come to town.
Besides, we're all a bunch of "characters."

I'm glad, it's "characters"-
God favors.

"Characteristically" yours, *Terry R. Morehouse*

Chapter 54

HER NAME WAS BLANCHE

Her name was Blanche.

I'm not too sure how old she was, 75, 80, perhaps.

It's not important really.

Blanche was a long-time member of this little Lutheran church,

Where Kansas winds had always seemed to blow

The people gathered round the council table were her fellow members.

She'd known them all her life. Since they were young,

They had shared the eucharist together.

When the meeting ended, she asked us all to sit right down.

There was something on her mind, she said,

And in her heart.

"Am I responsible for Mary's death?" she asked.

Tears began to flow.

You see, her best friend, Mary, died last summer.
On that very day, she and Blanche had been together.
It was only later, Mary's son implied,
That if it hadn't been for Blanche,
and their little trip to town that day,
Mary wouldn't have died.

For almost three months---she lived those penetrating words;
Hour after hour, long into the night, she heard them spoken.
Over and over and over again, she sobbed herself to sleep.
Wondering, "Could they be true?"
Her best friend Mary.

Then, as if on signal, came the gasp of all the others.
'Blanche'--was showered with their grace, their reassuring
love,
And in the wonder of their words,
their hugs, their tears of caring,
there came a blessed assurance.
For Blanche, their dear, dear friend.

I felt the breath of Jesus, God's shalom,
Blowing still, beneath those prairie winds.
(*Terry R. Morehouse, October 1981*)

Chapter 55

FROM OUT OF THE BLUE

"Good morning, Mr. Morehouse!"
She was such a tiny thing,
A little girl who lived close by,
And I didn't know her name.

But she knew mine!
I said, "Good Morning!"
As I continued on my morning jog,
But wished I knew HER name!

I have to say --I smiled--all the way back home.
I wondered if she knew how good she made me feel.

For there is something in a name,
In hearing it, politely, and respectfully,
From out of nowhere.
There is something in a name, and knowing--
That it's yours!

How we long to feel that way—
To believe we matter just enough,
To have someone say our name.

Do we understand the depth of feelings such as these?
That from the vastness of an unsuspecting morning,
A little girl spoke our name?

Thank God she came along. I won't forget.
(*Terry R. Morehouse, 1988*)

Chapter 56

WITH GOD ON MY SIDE

She had won the race!
She would wear the gold!
She would feel the accolades of her country, her world!
She would stand before all,
With joy in her heart, as her flag unfurled!

"How did that happen?" folks wanted to know.
"I guess...I had God on my side,"
She shyly surmised.

As I heard, it, I wondered as I watched.
Do people ever think about words like these?

On her side today, but not with the others?
Is the God of our faith, as fickle as fate?
Is God on the side of winners alone?
What must I do to have God on my side?
Or not do,

When not there tomorrow?

There is a message from heaven that shatters all that.
It sounds like a cry,
It looks like a cross.
Like a rock,
That was once rolled away.

God---on our side, in winning *and* losing.
Thank God, it's not just for today!

Chapter 57

TO JOYCE AND CLARENCE

I can't imagine what it's like to lose your child.
As I sat there in the church today,
  Those were my thoughts,
  That was my pain.
How could I ever know what you are feeling?
  Will your pain of losing never end?

To slip into your sadness--To feel what you are feeling,
  Is impossible.
Only tiny, tiny, glimpses now and then, are mine.
  If I put another name, another face, to David's,

One of my own, a Shelly, Amy, or Kristina,
Perhaps then. But still just, a tiny, tiny, touch
Of the darkness that you feel,
Is mine.
The movie of his life was played before you,
His friends, the actors, and the actresses,
His brothers and their families,
And you.
The music of the soundtrack was his own,
His, the drumbeat and the drummer.
Your son.
He lived today, he lives tomorrow,
In the melody, the music,
And the song.
His laughter, and the love that was his life--
Will tremble through the walls,
Down the hallways and the stairs,
Inside of you, forever.
David was a gift, that can't be grasped,
But oh, if only it could.
If only it could.
He and Kirk will wait for you, with all the saints.
And with the maestro of the music
Of the universe.
Alleluia, and amen.
(Dedicated to Joyce and Clarence Pedersen, October 30, 1998)

Chapter 58

JOAN

Our love has weathered.
   Tides of time
   Have etched their lines
   In each of us.
Still separate and alone,
   Yet the texture
   Of our separateness,
   Has made us stronger
   In togetherness.
I know that I've been hard to understand,
   But you've reached inside of me,
   Nurturing…the me I didn't know was there.
I'm still a hopeless dreamer,
   Sometimes a "plain old poop,"
But you've accepted part of me
   That even I don't understand.

Our love has blended,
　Like the colors of the rainbow.
　Deepening,
　As the contrast of the clouds and sunshine
　Come together.
Even with the ever-changing seasons,
There waits—a hopefulness of tomorrow's dawn.

I love you.

Chapter 59

MYSTERIOUS WAYS

"You just have to say…it was the case of God—working,
   Through the skill of the surgeon."

Those were the husband's words,
   When a tiny, dangerous, bleeding artery,
   Was clamped—successfully.
It had threatened her life!

And so, it was—God—working, through the surgeon.
For those who have eyes to see.
For those—who see with the eyes of faith.

Others may say—it was not God at all,
   But science, and skill, technology and training--made possible
By human kind.

Mysterious ways, these ways of God.

If she died, what then?
God sleeping,
Not caring?
Not there?
Or not enough faith?

Or—caring more deeply
Than we will ever be able to go.
It all depends
On how you see.

Thanks, O Lord…
For working through the skillful hands,
The caring hearts, of humankind.
With greater skill than we will ever know. Amen

Chapter 60

IN THE PASTOR'S STUDY
WITH THE 23ᴿᴰ PSALM

It's quiet here this morning,
   the gentle hum
   of the refrigerator,
   the soft tick-tocking
   of the clock
   the only sounds surrounding.

Time...tick-tocking on,
   waiting, as they say,
   for no one.
The old shepherd Psalm
   Is there before me.
   I've read it to others,
   so many times, as their lives
   wound down,

And their time ran out.

I've studied it so
    as to teach it to others.
But what does it say to *me?*
    This time
    To my time and me?

My shepherd,
    Where are you in my life today?
    And where are you leading me?
    To greener pastures?
    Or beside the quiet waters?
    Or through the darkest valleys?
    Or to none of the above?
"You are with me"
    That's the key.
    Let me not forget, O Lord,
    That you are with ME.
That your mercy and goodness
    Will follow me.
    My whole life long! *(Terry R. Morehouse, 1993)*

Chapter 61
A PRAYER FOR A
WORLD THAT'S CHANGING

Lord…someone said it's going to be an early winter.
The birds are bunching up already.

They could be right, the signs are written
     On the sumac and the maples.
The brilliant reds are lighting up the forests, even now.

But I'm not sure I'm ready, Lord!
Isn't there something you could do to slow this world down?
Kids are off to school,
Some of them to college!
One of them is mine!

I'm just not sure I'm ready for all of this, Lord.
I'm still a college kid myself at heart.

Times are changing,
And I guess they're going to change,
Despite the way I feel.

So, help me Lord.
Let the winds of change blow gently in my soul.
Let the joys be kissed,
The roses smelled,
The colors loved.

Allow the changelessness of Your eternal presence,
To calm my fears, give me confidence
For each new season of my life,
Whatever that may bring.

(Terry R. Morehouse, September 1985)

Chapter 62

A CHRISTMAS HIP

A pastor was home at Christmas.
  Confined to the walls
  With an afghan shawl
  Around him!

The need for a hip had started this trip,
  At this holy time
  Of year.

Could the world, would the world,
  Should the world, survive?
  Holy smokes alive!
  Could he?

After thirty years of frantic cheer,
  Delivering sermons
  In rapid succession,

Counseling others, and private confessions,
   He had hardly had time
   For his own depression!

Ah yes! Tis true, believe it!
   Twas not his demise
   But to his surprise, the Spirit
   Came into their lives.

Like a dove, from above,
   Came the Christ,
   In love.

And the pastor wasn't in charge!

Chapter 63

WACO TEXAS - APRIL 1993

Why do people continue to believe, Lord?
  Thomas did, because he'd seen the place
  Where the nails had entered,
  The wounds still lingered, in your Son.

"Blessed are those, who have not seen, yet still believe,"
  You tell us. Yet oftentimes,
  We see too much.

When Jonestown hit the news, I thought we would have
learned.
  I couldn't imagine that it all might happen
  Once again.

Now it had. In Waco, Texas. Ninety people lay there, in the
rubble.
  Victims of a twisted mind, their leader,
  And their god.

Why do people still believe? There are so many reasons not to.

Help us on our weary way, O God.
Forgiving, once again, our foolishness,
As you did once upon a cross.

How long, O Lord, how often,
Must you die for us?

Have mercy on us all!

Chapter 64

WHEN TRUST IS BROKEN

When I think about the story of my life,
The memories of a shattered trust
   Still haunt me.

I've been the "breaker" and the "broken."
Speaking just for me,
   I'm not quite sure which can hurt the worst.

When trust is broken, dear God,
What then? Where **do** you go?
From the tears, you've left behind?

How can we begin again?
Can all the little pieces of the puzzle
  Ever fit together as they were?

No one knows how much it hurts
Except the ones

Who've seen it slip away.

"Where is chapter two, we pray?"

"Forgiveness" and "rebuilding,"
  I know no other way.

This chapter two? It is the longest,
And the hardest ever.

It often takes a lifetime to rebuild.

"Love," they say, must bear all things,
Hope all things, endure.
    It is the way of Christ.

Memories will linger, they never go away.
The hope for healing only comes,
    From the tissue of the scar.

Chapter 65

A WORLD WITHOUT
COKE AND CHIPS

Have you ever wondered how our world would
  Be without Coke and chips?
I know the farmers would be delighted
  To have us drinking milk again.

I am, have always been, a self-confessed,
  "Junk food junkie" of the highest order.
(Just ask the kids whom they like to shop with,
  For something REALLY good to eat!)

So, you can imagine me to be
  A pretty anxious fellow
When I arrived at this retreat.
  It was a place, where only "healthy" foods were eaten.
Nothing else could be consumed---by folks who visit here.

The question was, could I survive?

The question is, did I?
I must confess, I never planned to try.

Hidden in my car,
    In the corner of my trunk,
I had tucked a box of Pringles, and a can of diet Coke.
    In the later afternoon, I tiptoed out to get them,
Just to calm my nerves.

I felt quite guilty.
    In my room, I quickly locked my door.
But ohh! They were so good!
Besides, a guy just can't be holy
    All the time! "Right, Lord?"
    (Heh, heh!)
"Pass the chips, Lord?"
(Private Retreat-ARC-Cambridge, MN)

Chapter 66

THE FIRST STEP

John Shea—I think it was,
      Who said,
   "The first step toward spirituality
         Is to notice."
   Of course!
   How simple…
   But how quickly we forget.

To notice, how the tulip bulbs are bulging up,
Even as the snow is flying.

Notice—two men in a restaurant booth.
      One is wearing cowboy boots,
         Both are wearing business suits and ties.
   Both are working seriously
      To complete the morning crossword puzzle.
   Notice—how your life-long friend and you,
      Have begun to think alike,

Read each other's minds,
Complete each other's sentences.
Notice—that the muskrat's back, doing things that musk-
rats do.
Notice—not the ugliness this time,
But the grace notes in your life.

The gentle ways the Spirit speaks, urges you,
Flirts with you,
As lovers often do.
Notice that you're alive, a child of God's
Who holds this world out to you.
To simply, irrepressibly,
Notice.

Chapter 67

A MORNING WALK

I took a morning walk the other day.

It was a time to listen--
  To the windchimes in the summer breezes,
  The rhythm of the waves upon the shore.
I heard—
  The busy chatter of the birds and squirrels
  A lonely sounding loon cry
  In the distance.

They are so hushed
  I hardly ever hear them.
  They run so deep, you see,
  That only if I really listen,
  Do they speak their truths to me.

They are, the sounds of many days and years.
   Tangled
   In a complicated life style
   That hardly ever takes the time
   To listen anymore.

Risks--
   Not taken.
   Dreams undreamed.
   Values compromised.
   Gifts too wonderful to bear.
The untouched mysteries of a waiting wilderness.

O Spirit of these mystic silent places,
   Speak! And let your servant hear.
   These yearnings of my heart,
   Have anguished there,
I pray Thee, let me hear!
   Let them speak their complicated truths to me.
(Terry R. Morehouse, 1994)

Chapter 68

BUTTERFLIES

I sat and watched the butterflies,
  And wondered what they do.

They simply seemed to flit,
  Then flap their wings,
  From time to time,
  For the longest time,
  Without a sound.
Then pause, then flit,
  Then flap,
  They're off again.

They must be doing good it seems.
Could a butterfly be mean?